THE INTERCESSORS

THE INTERCESSORS

by Denzil Holman

The Intercessors

Denzil R. Holman

Hazelwood, MO 63042-2299
Printing History: 1991, 1995

Cover Design by Tim Agnew

All Scripture quotations in this book are from the King James Version of the Bible unless otherwise identified.

Printed in United States of America

Printed by

Library of Congress Cataloging-in-Publication Data

Holman, Denzil, 1940-
The intercessors / Denzil R. Holman.
p. cm.
ISBN 0-932581-68-4 :
1. Intercessory prayer—Pentecostal churches. 2. Pentecostal churches—Doctrines. 3. Christian life—Pentecostal authors.
I. Title.
BV215.H64 1990
248.3′2—dc20 90-39538
CIP

To my wife, Eva, and my children
for their loyal support and encouragement
while I was writing this book

Contents

Foreword

The twenty-three chapters of Brother Denzil Holman's first book on prayer, entitled *Conquest Through Prayer,* let us know that Brother Holman is more than an author; he knows something about praying. And now he has written another book on the subject, *The Intercessors.*

God may pass by our elaborate programs and outstanding talents, but He will never pass by the prostrate form of an intercessor. Intercession is the ultimate in unselfishness. It is truly following in the steps of Jesus.

An intercessor is a go-between in the best sense of the word. He is one who pleads to God on behalf of a needy person or persons. He must love both parties. The consecration of an intercessor is beautiful.

An even higher level of intercession is reached when "we know not what we should pray for as we ought: but the Spirit itself maketh intercession for us with groanings which cannot be uttered" (Romans 8:26). This kind of praying takes place only in and through those who passionately want to pray. The Holy Spirit will not accomplish this phenomenon through prayerless, unconcerned people.

We need this kind of praying because of our human ignorance: "for we know not what we should pray for." The manifestation of this kind of praying is "groanings which cannot be uttered," but these groanings are perfectly intelligible to God.

The purpose of Brother Holman's writing on this needed subject is to inspire many of us who will "stand in the gap" and pray for our perishing generation. Individuals, cities, nations, and the world can be changed when we reach the level of intercession in our praying.

Prayer is a lifetime school, because we can always learn more about it. We can learn from reading, but reading alone is not sufficient. We must practice as we read.

Jeremiah was one of the choice intercessors of the Old Testament. One day he bellowed out in agony of soul, "Oh that my head were waters, and mine eyes a fountain of tears, that I might weep day and night for the slain of the daughter of my people!" (Jeremiah 9:1). May his example inspire us today.

C. M. Becton

Preface

There is an innate desire within the heart of every dedicated child of God to be used in His service in some way. It is a natural reaction for those who have been redeemed by the precious blood of Jesus to desire to render to God something in return for His amazing grace.

One of the ways in which we can serve the Lord is by serving others in intercessory prayer. When we have served the least, we have served Him. There is always a need for more to enlist in this vital area of the kingdom of God.

It is my desire and prayer that this book will help more of God's people to be aware of the need in this area and give them a greater knowledge of intercession. I hope that these words will awaken compassion and concern in people's hearts and motivate them to cry out in prayer, "Lord, make me an intercessor."

In order to have the harvest of souls that Jesus died for and our hearts yearn for, we must dramatically increase the number of intercessors in the church. As our preachers declare the Word of God from the pulpits and our saints witness to the lost outside the walls of our churches, we need intercessors to labor in prayer.

Lest anyone should misunderstand, I am not writing from an attitude of spiritual superiority. For many years I have focused on prayer in my teaching and preaching. It seems that the Lord has directed my ministry in that sphere of study and experience. The longer I am in the ministry the more I become aware of how little we know about prayer. But God is helping us as we sincerely desire to know Him better. This book was born out of a burdened heart, and I want to share with others information and experiences that may help the cause of God.

I want to thank the Lord for the inspiration to write. Without His anointing on my pencil and typewriter, I would be helpless and ineffective.

I also want to thank my wife, Eva, and my children for their support and encouragement, as I have spent much time alone in my office while writing. They have unselfishly allowed me to give myself to the ministry of writing because they knew that God wanted me to do it and that it meant much to me. They have often been sounding boards for some thought or inspiration that I shared with them first.

I would like to express my gratitude to the Editorial Division, the Executive Publication Committee, and the Pentecostal Publishing House for providing an outlet for me to express my burden through the writing ministry.

Special thanks goes to the various ones who have provided material that I have used for testimonies, analogies, and illustrations in this book. Time and space do not allow me to mention all of the names of those who contributed.

As you read this book, I hope you will be inspired and motivated to become an intercessor. Many of you are already being used in intercessory prayer, and I trust that this writing may help you to be even more effective. Any positive results of this book will come because Jesus Christ, our Great Intercessor, has performed the work. To God be all the glory forever.

Chapter One

The Call to Prayer

The still small voice of God arrested me in my tracks as I reached into the front seat of my car. I was getting ready to leave for work and had gone to my car to get something. The words pierced through my soul as the Lord said to me, "My people have forgotten me for days without number." I could feel in my spirit, it seemed, the very sadness and grief that God was feeling at being ignored. As I began to meditate upon this message, the Lord let me know that in many cases His people had gone for long periods of time without meaningful prayer being part of their daily life. Countless days and weeks had slipped by without some of His children consulting Him or including Him in their lives and plans.

As I drove down Black Canyon Freeway that morning, I began to repent for the wasted opportunities when I could have prayed. Tears blurred my vision and ran down my cheeks in rivulets as remorse gripped my soul. I repented for my neglect in not giving the Lord more time in prayer.

God is calling us to prayer as never before. Prayer has always been a necessity for spiritual survival and growth. It has always been a prerequisite to revival. But the late hour in God's prophetic time clock and the billions of souls make us realize soberly that prayer must be a priority.

There is a hunger and spiritual restlessness among us. We are discovering afresh the adventure of praying in a deeper way. Across our fellowship all-night prayer meetings and round-the-clock prayer chains are becoming more numerous. We are finding that the more we pray, the more we want to pray. Saints are rising early and coming to the churches for prayer before going to work. Youth groups are meeting for prayer instead of traditional youth activities. Something is happening. God is calling us to prayer.

Our spiritual leaders have their fingers on the pulse of God and are in tune with His heartbeat. They are directing us down the path of revival, which leads through the prayer rooms. There is a clarion call from the Lord to give ourselves, ministers and laity alike, to prayer.

The Scriptures mandate that we pray. We have no other option; we must pray. If we do not, we will lose our own souls, and we will not reach the unsaved.

Many people are discovering that prayer is not a bitter pill as they supposed. Instead, they are finding that prayer can be exciting, thrilling, and wonderful. There are heights of joy and ecstasy in the prayer closet. There are feelings of rapture and glory in communing with the Lord.

We do not pray because it is in vogue but because a hunger for more of God causes our souls to ache. Through repentance and heart searching, we rend our hearts as Joel 2:13 commands.

Prayer is more than mere words spoken in a conversation with God. It is more than words printed in ink on paper. Prayer is a relationship with the Lord. In prayer we talk to Someone, namely God, who really exists, and we become involved in a heart-to-heart relationship with Him.

When we compare the needs of the world today to the fires of revival that swept across the people and nations of the first century and the mighty miracles of the Book of Acts, we become acutely aware of our need for the same power that the early church possessed. And the Lord is calling us to prayer. Through earnestly seeking after God, we will receive the power of God to help us fulfill the great commission.

There is no wholesale price available on the power of the Holy Spirit. All great spiritual endeavors begin with prayer. Though many of us have been on this pilgrim journey for a number of years, we sense the need for a greater move of God to reach our generation.

Many people who attend church have not formed the habit of prayer, even though they obeyed the message of salvation, being baptized in Jesus' name and receiving the Holy Spirit. While they pray over their food and before they go to sleep at night, some have missed the joy of effective and meaningful communion with Jesus.

The call to prayer takes us to a place of heart searching and consecration. We must have a fresh renewing of the Holy Spirit in our own personal walk with God. We must pray until the wells of living water flow freely in our souls. The living water that Jesus spoke about in John

4:14 will cleanse us, driving out pollutants and carnality that would impede the flow. Out of our innermost being will flow rivers of living water (John 7:38), which will affect us and also those who come in contact with us.

With personal renewal, spiritual vision becomes clearer. Eyes are opened to the needs around us. Deep, heart-rending prayer makes us sensitive to the needs of people. Our attention is diverted from ourselves to others.

And that brings us to the subject of this book, intercessory prayer, which is praying for others. Through intercessory prayer, we can make a difference in the lives of others. In fact, God depends upon us to pray for others. He challenges us to become intercessors.

Chapter Two

Making Up the Hedge

"And I sought for a man among them, that should make up the hedge, and stand in the gap before me for the land, that I should not destroy it: but I found none" (Ezekiel 22:30).

When Joshua led the Israelites into Canaan, God went before them and fought for them. He performed mighty miracles, even superseding the natural laws of the solar system, to aid them. After the battles were over, the land was divided among the twelve tribes of Israel. It was further subdivided as each family was given its parcel for an inheritance. It was a gift to them from a gracious God, and God had reminded them in Deuteronomy 6 that they should ever be mindful of His goodness to them. Since the Israelites were chiefly pastoral and agricultural, their land was very important to them, and they guarded and used it carefully. For example, in accordance with God's law, Naboth refused to sell his family inheritance even to the king. (See I Kings 21.)

Around the perimeters of their vineyards, the landowners often built a barrier for safety and privacy. It was typically a wall or a hedge, and it insured that wild beasts or thieves would not have easy access to the vineyard. The landowner would cultivate and manicure his parcel of land until it was almost a work of art. If a section of the wall crumbled or a portion of the hedge was destroyed, the owner or someone he designated would make up the gap in the hedge or wall to keep out intruders until he could repair the breach.

Definition of an Intercessor

An intercessor is like an ancient guard who stood in the gap and made up the hole in the hedge or wall. He seeks to protect the well-being of another person. He stands in the middle between two people or between people and God and pleads their cause.

Inter is a prefix meaning "between, in the midst, intervening between, existing between." To *intercede* is to intervene between parties with a view toward reconciling differences. *Intercession* is the act of interceding. An *intercessor* is someone who participates in the act of intercession.

Intercessory prayer involves an individual with a need, whether spiritual or physical; God, who hears prayer and can meet the need; and a third party, the intercessor, who pleads the needy person's cause.

Here are some examples of intercessory prayer: A minister anoints a sick person with oil and prays for healing. A mother prays for her unsaved children, who are not praying for themselves; she stands between the loved ones and God, asking for God to work in their lives and draw them to salvation. A pastor prays for the lost in the city where he pastors a church, standing in the gap between them and a holy God who cannot tolerate sin and pleading with God to save them. A terrible tragedy is about to befall one of God's children when suddenly and unexplainably another saint of God feels a burden to pray and makes up the hedge by asking God to intervene and avert a tragic event. A church unites in prayer, taking prayer requests to the throne of grace.

Simply put, intercession is praying for the needs of another, or on behalf of another.

Intercession does not mean we automatically receive everything we desire. God is sovereign and has a definite will and purpose. We cannot make God bow to our every whim and desire; He will perform His will. Moreover, God will not violate His written Word no matter how long and earnestly we pray. And in the matter of salvation God will not violate a person's own will and choice. Even though we pray for the salvation of others, they will not be saved until they choose to come to God. Because of our intercession, however, God will deal with their hearts and woo them to Him. He will use events to lead them to a place of decision. Many souls have come to God because a loved one continually brought them before God in prayer. God dealt with their soul, and eventually they surrendered their life to Him.

We must have a balance in our prayer. We should give a portion of our prayer time to praise and worship. If needed, we should allow time for repentance. Part of our prayer time should consist of meditation and part should consist of petition, which is asking for requests. And then intercession should comprise a good portion of our prayer. We will often mingle petition with intercession as we make requests for the needs of others.

Why Does God Work through Intercessory Prayer?

After having been in the church and in the ministry for many years, I began to ask myself one day, Why does God work through the avenue of intercessory prayer? He is God and knows everything. No need escapes His attention and knowledge. He sees every sparrow that falls, so surely He knows every need that His children have. And since He sees and knows everything, when one of His children faces an emergency, He could go ahead and handle the crisis without notifying another saint to pray about it.

In many situations, God does see a need and dispatches angels to the rescue. In other cases, God handles the problem by His Spirit. In situations like this, we often do not realize that God has spared our lives or performed a miracle. We may have no knowledge of an accident that never happened or a disease that was nipped in the bud. Nevertheless, God in His providence reached down and remedied the situation.

Since God is sovereign, He can handle a situation in any way that He sees fit. He does not have to answer to us, because He is God. Of course, God does operate according to principles of His Word, and whatever He does is always right and just. But His ways and His thoughts are often above and beyond our human reasoning.

One of the reasons that God chooses to involve His church in the process of answering prayer is that God thereby gets glory and honor. If God does a miracle but people have no knowledge of it, then they do not praise Him for it. When members of God's church join in intercessory prayer, however, and receive an answer, they praise Him and He gets glory. When they testify to others about the miracle He gets glory again.

Another reason why God uses the avenue of intercession to answer prayer is that God uses His body, the church, to fulfill His will on the earth. He is the Head of the church, and we are members of His body. For example, God is aware of a need somewhere because He is omniscient, and He sends a message to a member of His body to pray for that need. The person He uses may receive His message in the form of a burden to pray, or a still, small inner voice, or another means. When the person prays to God on behalf of the need, then God supplies the answer.

If God has burdened an individual to pray for a particular need, it is obvious that it is the will of God to answer that need. If not, why would God burden a saint to pray for a particular need? When the answer comes, God gets glory for performing the miracle. God could dispatch an angel and bypass humanity, which He does in some cases. But God likes to work through the church, the body of Christ. We then give Him glory, praise, and thanksgiving.

When God works through the avenue of intercession to perform miracles and supply the needs of individuals, our faith is strengthened. And the Lord wants us to have faith in Him. Without faith it is impossible to please Him (Hebrews 11:6). Faith becomes stronger through use, much like muscles in the human body.

Intercessory prayer is an ideal way to be laborers together with God. God has chosen to accomplish many of His divine works and acts by our intercessory prayers. As members of His body, when Christ, the Head, sends direction, we should carry out His signals and desires. In this way we can have a part with God in His works. All the glory belongs to Him, and we rejoice in being used by Him.

Intercession Is an Opportunity for Service

Our intercession is the link between the needs of people and a God who knows no limitations and has inexhaustible resources. In some situations, we may be the only human who knows of a particular need. What an opportunity for service! How dare we seal our lips and not intercede? We must take full advantage of the opportunities for service to God and others.

One of the great privileges granted to us as children of the Lord is the opportunity to approach Him at any time. We do not have to wait for an engraved invitation or a particular time. We have a standing invitation to enter the throne room anytime as long as we meet His conditions. As long as we come in faith, with a clean heart, and ask according to His will, we can come with boldness. (See Hebrews 4:16.)

Not only are we invited to come anytime, but God desires that we come to Him. We do not have to make an appointment or wait until a certain time. He desires for us to come to Him in prayer.

Intercessory prayer is an opportunity not only to save lives, but eternal souls. By standing in the gap and making up the hedge, we can influence souls to turn to God when they are on a collision course with death and destruction. Our intercession can mean the difference in people's lives being spared and their being able to continue working here for God.

No one is excluded from this opportunity. Age, education, financial status, and social level cannot restrict an individual from this opportunity. Intercessors include senior citizens, children, young adults, and people in mid life. The ranks contain preachers, housewives, salesmen, truck drivers and missionaries as well as people in hundreds of other occupations.

What honor God has bestowed upon us by allowing members of His church to be involved in the process of answering prayers! What a humbling experience for God to trust us with a burden of intercessory prayer to pray for someone's needs!

It is also a great responsibility. We must feel the responsibility keenly enough to pursue relentlessly onward in the closet of prayer until we feel the answer has come.

Intercession provides an opportunity for true fulfillment and purpose in living. Through intercessory prayer we can express in a small way the gratitude that we feel towards God. It is one way we can present our bodies as a living sacrifice. (See Romans 12:1.)

The Importance of Intercession

Just as the guard who stood in the gap in the vineyard perimeter hedge in biblical days played a vital role, so the intercessor today fills a place of great importance in the work of God.

We must have God-called preachers and teachers to declare the Word of God. We will always need the preaching and teaching of the Word to save and keep us. And there are other positions of leadership in the church that are vital and necessary. But no position in the kingdom of God is more important than the intercessor, the prayer warrior. We may have the well-oiled machinery of local church organization. Our music departments may be of the highest quality. Our outreach programs may fill our pews with visitors. But it is essential to have precious soldiers who will lie prostrate before God in intercessory prayer. Otherwise our efforts will fall short of God's optimum for us.

A leading minister, once visited a church to consider becoming its pastor. He asked his wife how the ladies prayer meeting went that day. He wanted to know how the people prayed and if they really knew how to pray. He knew that if it was a praying church, it would have revival and growth.

Some people who lack musical talent or other more visible talents excel in the prayer rooms. As a pastor, I would prefer to have the intercessor if I had to make a choice of one or the other. I am a musician and love good music, but I am aware of the importance of the prayer warrior in the kingdom of God. If God uses someone in a ministry of prayer, he should not feel unimportant to God. He should be clothed in humility but understand that he is a key person in the function of the church. The intercessor should not take his role lightly. God depends on him and so does the church.

When I hear of a child of God killed in an accident, I have at times asked myself did someone fail to pray. We must not discount the will of God in such cases, for only God knows when it is His will for such a thing to happen. But could it be possible at times that God burdened someone to pray for an impending disaster and the individual shrugged it off and failed to pray? We must realize the importance of intercession when God places a burden of prayer upon us.

Pastor Larry Flenniken of Sherman, Texas, is an example of the importance of intercession. On February 4, 1967, he was in Vietnam at a time when he was not serving God. The following account by him has been excerpted from the December 1988–February 1989 issue of the *Outreach* and edited:

"There are three men in each company who have to know the location of the company at all times and are marked by the PRC 25 radio they carry. Their life expectancy in combat is forty-five seconds. I was one of them. Within thirty seconds from the first round, a recoilless rifle marked my position, and the first round literally blew me twelve to fifteen feet. As I became aware of the surrounding conditions I began to crawl to a place of cover. We had not had time to dig in, but just a few feet away I found a crevice in the ground, which I crawled into head first. As I had been hit in the back, blood ran down the small of my back, around my neck, and into my mouth. This almost made me panic, for I thought I was bleeding internally.

"At that point I asked God to have mercy and find an intercessor somewhere. Halfway around the world, at that very time, the United Pentecostal Church where my parents and wife attended was having its midweek Bible study. Without any means of communication from the Republic of Vietnam to Flint, Michigan, except the Holy Spirit, my mother in an orderly way told the pastor, Brother Robert McKinnies, that she felt an urgency, felt a spirit of heaviness and weeping. Immediately God confirmed this to the pastor, and he called the whole church to prayer. There was a great spirit of weeping as the people began to intercede in prayer."

As a result, Larry Flenniken's life was spared, and God led him to salvation.

God truly works in miraculous ways to perform His works. The church cannot operate at its optimum without people who are sensitive to the voice of God and who allow Him to use them in intercessory prayer. Intercessors are vital and necessary to the work of God.

Chapter Three

Intercessors in the Bible

The Bible records many examples of unselfish people who were intercessors in their generation. They give us examples to follow. In this chapter we will examine the lives of some of these intercessors who left an indelible mark forever on many people.

The Word of God is more than a history book or an account of the Israelites and their relationship with God. Its stories teach lessons that are applicable today. By their example the intercessors of the Bible show us how we can involve ourselves in the same unselfish service of intercessory prayer.

Abraham is a key figure in the Old Testament as well as for all time. He was called a friend of God and the father of the faithful. He had an unshakable faith in God and a heart of compassion for others. He went out of his way to be patient and kind to his nephew, Lot, and gave him first choice of the land when it became obvious that they needed to part ways. Lot settled in Sodom and arose to a place of prominence in the city at about the same time as God decided to bring judgment upon it for the sins of its citizens. Since Abraham was His friend, God revealed His intention to him. Abraham interceded for Lot and the city, pleading for the Lord to spare it. Finally, the Lord promised to spare Sodom if He found ten righteous souls in the city. Although there were not ten righteous souls, God did deliver Lot and his family from the destruction.

This story gives us an insight into the longsuffering of God. The Lord will go to great lengths to spare lost humanity. This truth encourages us to intercede for souls even when we feel that there is little hope for them.

Moses was a very patient man. He led an enormous multitude of people toward the land of Canaan. His love for them after their repeated murmuring and complaining is a testimony to the kindness of Moses as well of God. When God planned to bring judgment upon the Israelites for their unbelief and disobedience, Moses showed the spirit of an intercessor. He stood between them and God, pleading their cause. (See Numbers 14.)

Interceding for the lost necessitates loving the sinner while hating his sin. In intercession we have to look past the sometimes nasty and unpleasant personalities of people and pray for them with compassion, though they may be very unlovable in many ways.

Moses exemplified the pastor who will weep and shed tears over backsliders and wayward saints whom he loves dearly. Such a pastor will plead with God to reserve judgment and extend mercy a little longer. Like Moses pleading for Israel, many a godly parent has interceded for lost children, and God has answered their cries of parental concern.

The high priest fulfilled the role of an intercessor when he went into the Holy of Holies on the Day of Atonement yearly to sprinkle the blood on the mercy seat. He was a type and shadow of Jesus Christ, who went behind the veil for us and ever lives to be our intercessor. The high priest could feel with compassion and empathy the desperate plight of the people who were helpless to extricate themselves from the handcuffs of sin, for he was under the same bondage as they were. He felt keenly his responsibility to do everything properly in the Tabernacle as the masses waited anxiously outside to know that God had accepted their sacrifice.

When we intercede for the lost, we can pray with compassion and sympathy, for once we were in the pit of sin also. We can remember the heartache and hopelessness of being bound by habits of sin that seem to have a viselike grip. If it were not for the grace of God, we would still be in the miry clay also.

The high priest could sense the bruised and broken hearts of the people as he fulfilled his role. People today have many deep hurts and bruises in their souls also. As intercessors we must have compassion on them and feel their pain as we seek God for them.

Samuel was a beloved prophet in Israel who filled the place of an intercessor as he prayed for his people. (See I Samuel 7:5.) When the people demanded a king to be like other nations, Samuel wanted Israel to remain a theocracy. Though grieved in heart and soul, Samuel anointed Saul, the man God chose to be king. Samuel continued to intercede in prayer for his country and its people. He considered it a sin to fail to pray for them (I Samuel 12:23).

When Saul disobeyed God, God rejected him as king. Samuel was brokenhearted and cried unto the Lord all night (I Samuel 15:11). Samuel mourned for Saul for some time because he loved him.

God is looking for those who love their people enough to be an intercessor like Samuel. God desires for us to weep tears of intercession and concern over our nation and its people. This principle also encompasses our spiritual family, the church of the living God. God wants us to intercede for our people and their needs. As Samuel, who felt a responsibility before God for his people, we must feel the same weight today.

King David also served as an intercessor. He had numbered Israel and thereby displeased God (I Chronicles 21). God decided to send judgment upon Israel, but David stepped between them and judgment, pleading with God for mercy (verse 17). God sent an angel with a plague, and the angel drew his sword (verse 16). David interceded, built an altar unto the Lord, offered burnt offerings and peace offerings, and called upon the Lord. The Lord then commanded the angel to place his sword back in his sheath (verse 27).

This incident points out the importance of the intercessor. Judgment may be scheduled and on God's agenda until the intercessor steps forward and stays the hand of God. If someone is lost and God has burdened us to pray for him, we must not fail to intercede. We may save his life and soul.

Jeremiah is often called the weeping prophet. His heart was tender and he wept for the backslidden Israelites. He said, "Oh that my head were waters, and mine eyes a fountain of tears, that I might weep day and night for the slain of the daughter of my people!" (Jeremiah 9:1).

Our hearts must be touched by the needs of those we intercede for. Our prayers must not come from our lips only. Tears are the deepest expression of the heart and soul. When the heart is truly touched, the fountains open and tears spill down the face. Modern man says that it is not masculine to shed tears and that we should be strong and stoic. But we must not bottle up our love. Instead we should let love flow from within our souls by weeping for those we intercede for in prayer.

Nehemiah was an intercessor who prayed to God on behalf of the needs of Jerusalem. Though he was comfortable and materially at ease, his heart was touched by the plight of his people in their distant land (Nehemiah 1:4-11). He could have closed his mind and heart, asking, "Why should I be concerned with Jerusalem and her broken gates?" But he was willing to become involved. And the first step on the way was intercessory prayer.

We are safe in the fold. The Lord has brought us into the church. The Lord has taken care of our needs, both spiritually and physically. We can close our hearts to others and their needs, or we can be like Nehemiah and get involved. The lost need salvation, both at home and abroad. And the first step to reaching them is intercession.

Hezekiah was a godly king who did his best to turn the Israelites back to God and to destroy their idols. "He did that which was right in the sight of the LORD" (II Kings 18:3). He reestablished the observance of the Passover, leading the people in spiritual revival and renewal. His prayer of intercession for the people is recorded in II Chronicles 30:18. When the Assyrian army came to capture Jerusalem, after hearing of the Assyrian king's words against God, Hezekiah interceded for Jerusalem and God's people. Hezekiah understood that the enemy was attacking the honor of God and the heritage of Israel. God hearkened to Hezekiah's intercession and turned back the Assyrians, killing great numbers of them in one night. Their ruler, Sennacherib, returned to Assyria, where he was slain by one of his own sons.

The enemy seeks to destroy our heritage today, for he does not like our doctrine and holiness. He comes against the church with the temptation to compromise on our foundational beliefs. We must intercede for our youth so that they will have a love and appreciation for what has been given to them, lest the enemy take it away. We must also pray for the ministers who lead us so that God will deliver them from the wiles of the enemy.

Jesus, our supreme example, was an intercessor. He prayed many times by Himself and sometimes prayed all night. (See Mark 1:35; 6:46; Luke 5:16; 6:12.) He prayed for others as He healed them. He prayed for Peter that Satan would not destroy him (Luke 22:31-32). On the cross He prayed for the very ones who were killing Him: "Father, forgive them; for they know not what they do" (Luke 23:34).

John 17 records the intercessory prayer of Jesus just prior to His arrest and crucifixion. He first talked with His disciples, seeking to comfort and encourage them for the ordeal just ahead of them. Then He began to pray, and His prayer covered some key areas of their lives.

In verse 11 He said, "Keep through thine own name those whom thou hast given me, that they may be one, as we are." In this important prayer Jesus prayed for the unity of the brethren. For the church to accomplish the will of God, it must have unity.

In verse 15 Jesus said, "I pray not that thou shouldest take them out of the world, but that thou shouldest keep them from the evil." In our prayers of intercession for each other today we should likewise ask that God keep our brethren from worldliness and the attacks of the enemy.

In verse 17 Jesus prayed, "Sanctify them through thy truth: thy word is truth." We should pray that God will direct the ministry to preach to us the truth of the Word of God. The preached Word is part of the sanctifying and cleansing process.

In verse 20 Jesus prayed for those yet to come who would hear the Word and the witness of the apostles.

As He neared the end of His prayer, He prayed that we would reach heaven and behold Him in glory (verse 24). Jesus wants us all to be saved.

The apostle Paul made several references to intercessory prayer. He practiced intercessory prayer (Romans 1:9; 10:1; Philippians 1:4; Ephesians 1:16). He admonished us to involve ourselves in intercession also (Ephesians 6:18; Colossians 4:2-3; I Timothy 2:1).

James 5:16 instructs us all to be intercessors: "Pray one for another."

Chapter Four

Is There Not a Cause?

David asked this question shortly after Goliath roared his challenge to the Israelite soldiers, leaving them pale and full of fear. (See I Samuel 17:29.) David offered to fight the giant of Gath, but his brothers and others within earshot misunderstood him. His brothers accused him of pride, but David knew that more was at stake than just a skirmish between an Israelite soldier and a heathen opponent. The Philistines were attempting to bring reproach upon Jehovah, and David well knew of the delivering power of God. The backslidden and rejected monarch Saul cowered in fear like the rest of his men, but David with simple faith in God made his offer to fight this challenger who was reproaching his God. There was a cause as far as David was concerned, and he was willing to put everything, including his life, on the line for what he believed.

A cause is a belief, tenet, principle, conviction, ideal, purpose, or reason for being. Causes are usually born because of a need. Though this world will never become a utopia by human efforts, individuals who are dedicated to a cause can orchestrate significant changes in their sphere of interest.

Jonas Salk, a compassionate doctor, evidently grew weary of seeing young lives altered and destroyed by the scourge of polio and dedicated himself to the cause of research to find a polio vaccine. He gave himself tirelessly to his pursuit and changed many lives.

I asked a doctor who professes Christianity what motivates men and women to enter the medical profession. He answered that some enter it because of prestige, because of money, or because their father was a doctor, but many enter the field due to altruistic ideals. His own philosophy was that by being involved in the medical profession he was helping to ease the pain and suffering brought into the world by sin and Satan.

A cause ignites strong fires of zeal, fervor, and passion. It motivates people to the extreme limits of sacrifice as they give themselves for their convictions and ideals.

A cause often endures and is remembered long after those who initiated it have faded into obscurity. Many times the ones who sacrifice and give much to a cause remain forever anonymous. What is important is the cause they lived for and gave themselves to. The cause is greater than the recognition an individual may receive.

There is no greater cause than what we have as members of God's church. This cause originated from God Himself. From a heart of compassion for lost souls the love of God reaches down to save helpless sinners. Our cause is to reach out to the lost and perishing. The Lord Himself gave us the great commission, and that commission is to teach, preach, witness, and pray so that we may reap a worldwide harvest of souls.

Jesus lived with a sense of destiny even from childhood. At twelve years of age, the Father's business was already on His mind. He lived for a purpose, which was doing the will of the Father. He set His face towards accomplishing that cause and never wavered or flinched. As he approached the hour in which He would give His life as the supreme sacrifice for our redemption, He said, "For this cause came I unto this hour" (John 12:27).

Jesus fulfilled His mission on earth. He lived and died for His cause, which was to make salvation available to humanity. He then ascended to glory, leaving us with the responsibility of carrying out the work in our individual generations. The early church carried the torch in the first century. Now nineteen centuries later it is our generation and our day. And more people are alive today than ever before in the history of humanity. What an opportunity for evangelism!

Is there not a cause? Yes, there is a cause today. We are the people who have received the biblical revelation of the mighty God in Christ, baptism in Jesus' name, and the baptism of the Holy Spirit. We represent the greatest cause that has ever existed.

Along with preaching, teaching, and witnessing, an important element in fulfilling the will of God and accomplishing our mission is intercession. We must raise up more and more intercessors to reap a great harvest. God is looking to us, His church, to carry out His wishes and desires.

The cause is greater than any of us. We must commit ourselves to intercessory prayer. If people will toil and sacrifice for an earthly cause to alleviate physical suffering, surely we can do no less for this supreme cause. People have willingly risked their lives in world wars in order that their families and succeeding generations could have a life of democracy and freedom. May we present our bodies as a living sacrifice in order that others may know the joy of spiritual liberation and freedom from sin.

Paul told the Corinthian church, "And I will very gladly spend and be spent for you" (II Corinthians 12:15). Intercessory prayer is an opportunity to devote ourselves, spending ourselves for others.

People have been obsessed for a cause that was so fleeting. They have followed leaders that betrayed them later. They blindly followed after them like lemmings, dying on battlefields because a cause possessed and controlled them. A love for the lost must possess us so that we will be willing to sacrifice sleep, time, and energy to prostrate ourselves before God in intercession.

Intercessory prayer is the will of God. There is a strong scriptural foundation for intercession. God burdens people to pray for others. He responds to our prayers for others. This cause, which propels us to our knees and on our faces in prayer, is definitely the will and heartbeat of God.

Of course, we must do more than just pray. Some would like to pray only and let others do all the witnessing, working, giving, and so on. But it takes a balanced effort to reach the world with this message. We must elevate intercession to a place of importance, for without prayer we will utterly fail.

If this cause really burns within our hearts, there will be a willingness to pray. Multitudes of saints across the world are zealous and desirous of seeing the lost reached.

It seems that God is stirring all of us to a greater awareness of intercessory prayer in these closing hours of time.

People who work for a cause keep it ever before them as an incentive to press onward. In the long hours of laboring for a cause, it is easy to lose perspective of the ultimate purpose. But when a person grows weary, he can think of the benefits that will result from the combined efforts of many willing hands, and the cause will motivate him to keep pushing.

In the long, weary hours when we labor in prayer, it is important to keep our perspective. We must remember the spiritual benefits that lost souls will receive as a result of our labors together with God. We rally behind the cause that is associated with nail-scarred hands and feet and a riven side. The cause gives the added incentive that we need to press on a little longer and sacrifice a little more.

A proper awareness of the cause we represent and the importance of intercession to the overall effort is necessary for us to achieve the desired results. Intercession is definitely a vital part of God's plan to evangelize our world.

Chapter Five

We Can Change Our World

Each of us can have a lasting effect on our world. It is possible for each one of us, as individuals, to make an indelible mark on this generation. This truth should not inflate our ego and make us think more of ourselves than we ought to, but we should humbly recognize the potential when we allow God to work through us.

First, we must recognize that God deals with us on a one-to-one basis as individuals. Even when a preacher teaches and preaches to a congregation under the anointing and direction of God, he is speaking to individuals. We must each deal with God personally.

Each person is unique. Even the very hairs of our head are numbered (Matthew 10:30). Our fingerprints are different than everyone else's. Now scientists can make prints of our voices that are unique to us. Our facial features and numerous other characteristics distinguish us as individuals.

Jesus treated people as individuals during His earthly ministry. When He called the disciples to follow Him, it was a specific call directed to each of them personally. When the woman with the issue of blood touched Jesus, He focused His attention on her and singled her out. Even in crowds He often directed His words and deeds to individuals.

Jesus demonstrated the value He placed upon one person by visiting the woman at the well, the insane man of Gadara, and the diminutive Zacchaeus. He took the time to visit with Nicodemus and to call the rich young ruler. He gave a discourse on the value of individuals in Luke 15 when he talked about one lost sheep and one lost son.

The value of an individual is evident from the words of Jesus: "For what is a man profited, if he shall gain the whole world, and lose his own soul?" (Matthew 16:26). One person is so important that the angels rejoice when one sinner repents.

The Lord knew the potential in one person when He stopped Saul of Tarsus on the road to Damascus. God turned him around, and he became one of the mightiest missionaries of all time.

Each one of us can change the world because God hears and answers our prayers. He is no respecter of persons. God loves each of us as much as He loves everyone else. If we meet the conditions for effective prayer such as faith, obedience, and submission, God will answer. We can make things happen on our knees. We can cause God to act because we ask Him.

Our prayers have far-reaching influence in distance and time. Prayer has long arms that reach all the way to God's throne. We can speak our supplications and petitions to God, and through the power of God our prayers will produce results perhaps ten thousand miles away on another continent. The sound waves of a person's voice may not be heard outside his room, but God hears, and by His power He can touch someone across North America or the world.

If someone is a consistent prayer warrior, perhaps we can imagine a steady stream of heavenly signals beamed to heaven from his prayer closet. Perhaps God frequently dispatches angels because of his prayers to meet needs around the world. In an average suburban home or a farmhouse in the country, the prayer room becomes an important transmitting station of help because of the power of God through his intercession.

During World War II my grandmother had four sons on the battle fronts of the world at one time. Her sons were in the hotspots of Europe, and at least one was in the Battle of the Bulge. It was said that she could be found at night walking the sidewalks of Parkersburg, West Virginia, calling upon God to bring her boys home safely. God heard her prayers as she prayed in America, and the effects of her prayers were felt across the Atlantic.

The simple motto is so true: "Prayer changes things." Let us make it more personal by saying, "My prayer to God changes things."

We must understand that the power behind our prayer is the power of God; it does not originate from any human source. Prayer does not operate by extrasensory perception or psychic power that we use on God or others. Prayer is not merely positive thinking, positive confession, or a positive mental attitude. The positive mental attitude persuasion says, "I can do all things," but Paul said, "I can do all things through Christ." The power of prayer does not come from the human brain or spirit, but from God, who is sovereign in His use of power.

Prayer is not a hobby or something to play around with. We do not pray to get God to answer to our whims or play games. We must always be honest, be sincere, and have the right motives when we pray.

Prayer is powerful, and we must be responsible to direct our prayers properly. We must pray according to the will of God; God does not answer foolish, childish, selfish, or lustful whims. But people can bring difficulties upon themselves by praying insistently for certain things without carefully considering the will of God or the consequences of their requests. Israel cried to God for meat, and God sent them quail. But when the quail came, God also sent judgment because the people were so rebellious and filled with selfish lusts. (See Numbers 11.)

We can change our world by praying. Therefore, we must be spiritually mature in our requests while having childlike faith and simplicity of attitude.

The power of prayer is the power of God. It is beyond the capabilities of our finite minds to understand the power and resources of God. We cannot understand the size of a God who fills the farthest reaches of the solar system and beyond. We will always marvel at the handiwork of God in His creation and at the care He gives to detail.

At different times God has given us a glimpse of His power and glory through some visible manifestation. Of course we all know of His power by the experience of the Holy Spirit in our souls.

We must always remember that the power behind our prayers to change things in our world is not of human origin. It is the power of God, and without Him we can do nothing. It is humbling and awesome to see God answer our prayers and demonstrate His power.

Life is more than living a span of years and accumulating possessions, experiences, and knowledge. The body is more than food and clothing, and life is more than seeking after pleasure and satisfaction. True living comes from what we can contribute to the Lord and others through giving, sharing, and reaching out to help in a multitude of ways. We want to justify our existence. We want to feel that our life really matters.

One way to do so is through intercessory prayer. We can affect others by our prayers for them.

Our world begins with loved ones, friends, and neighbors, and then it reaches out to a widening circle of influence. It encompasses work associates and casual acquaintances. Like ripples on a pond, it reaches out to those in the city, the state, and then the nation. A burden can reach out to home missions and then across the seas to foreign missions. We can change our world at many levels of influence.

We can pray for other churches in a city and for the home missions churches across the state. Our prayers can reach out to the home missionary struggling in a metropolitan area like New York City. We can send the long arm of prayer to Singapore and Melbourne. We can shed tears for Frankfurt and Athens, and the power of God will lift our prayers and speed them on their way to produce results. We can change our world for God.

Some people have never journeyed more than a few hundred miles from home. They may live in a small community in mid America and never meet many people outside their geographical vicinity. But through intercessory prayer their lives can have a far-reaching effect and influence. Missionaries will feel spiritual support from a heavenly source and know that someone is praying for them somewhere, though they may never see them here face to face.

A weary and discouraged home missionary may be ready to give up and return to his home church dejected and beaten when strength and determination come to him from God when he sorely needs it. In another part of the country perhaps a prayer warrior felt a prayer burden to intercede for someone, and he touched God for that home missionary.

An evangelist and his wife may be traveling between revivals when they face certain disaster in the form of an automobile accident. At the last moment the power of God sweeps down and gently directs the automobile in a safer direction. God knew in advance about the crisis and perhaps burdened a saint somewhere to pray that morning for someone facing trouble.

We have in our possession the opportunity to be a blessing and to affect our world. We can live a cloistered, selfish life for ourselves or else live the unselfish life of service of one who gives himself to intercessory prayer. We can truly know the joy and fulfillment of being used by the Lord to bless others in this manner.

Chapter Six

A Labor of Love

The luthier cradled the partially finished guitar gently in his arms as he turned it over, looking for any hidden flaws that the overhead light might reveal. He had carefully chosen the wood for it with a keen eye trained by many decades of plying his trade. He had carved by hand the braces that supported the rim and soundboard. The rosewood sides and back were an object lesson in perfection. The solid spruce top that was the soundboard was selected after much deliberation. When the old guitar maker would finally be finished with his masterpiece, he wanted to be able to look at it with a sense of accomplishment.

It would not be a typical assembly-line guitar of the kind on display in most shops. The price alone would discourage most prospective buyers, for this fine instrument was made by a master craftsman as a labor of love. He was not a man who merely put in his eight hours daily. This was a man who loved the instrument, and his love was evident in what he produced.

The attitude of a typical worker towards his occupation will be revealed by the work that he produces. If he works for financial remuneration only and despises his work, it will be reflected in his quality control. If he works only from a sense of duty towards his employer and his family, his work will fall short of the optimum. But if an individual truly enjoys his work, whatever he produces, builds, or repairs will reflect his affection for his chosen occupation. Companies spend large sums of money for quality control because not everyone's work is a labor of love.

Nearly everything that we do has a motive behind it. Sometimes it is good to evaluate the driving force behind the things we do to see how appropriate our motive is. This is true with respect to prayer.

We should seek for our prayer lives to reach the fullest potential. We do not want our prayers to go unanswered or be deficient in their effectiveness. But if we pray only from a sense of duty or obligation, we will fall short of reaching our optimum. If we pray because we feel guilty and condemned when we do not pray, or if we pray only because our pastor makes us feel obligated, then we will cheat ourselves. We must not pray just to appease our conscience or because we feel that we are under legalistic bondage, for by so doing we will miss one of the joys of Christian living.

It is true that it is our duty and obligation to pray as believers. We are to present our bodies as a living sacrifice, and this is simply our reasonable service to God (Romans 12:1). Like the apostle Paul we are debtors to the lost (Romans 1:14). We are called to a life of service for the Lord and others. We are commanded to pray for others. But the motive for our intercession must go beyond duty alone; it should be a labor of love from our hearts.

When an individual is engaged in an activity or enterprise that he loves, it is not dull and boring. When a person is doing something he enjoys, time seems to flit away in a hurry. If we understand how to pray effectively and if we have a good relationship with the Lord, then prayer becomes a joy and a spiritual activity that we look forward to each day. The opportunity to intercede for others in prayer becomes an outpouring of love from our hearts, and time spent in prayer seems to go swiftly.

For our prayers to be effective, they must meet several important criteria. We must pray according to the will of God and the Word of God. (See I John 5:14-15.) We must have a repentant heart and pure heart. (See I John 3:20-22.) We must pray wholeheartedly. Our prayer must come from our heart and not merely our lips.

Sometimes when we begin to pray our heart may be on something else. For example, at church the pastor may ask everyone to stand and pray for a certain request, and we may be guilty of saying words when our mind is still on our job or the dirty dishes that we left at home. In such a situation we are praying from a sense of duty, obedience, and obligation but possibly not from the heart and soul of love.

But when we pray for another and our heart is in it, we go beyond duty, and our prayer becomes an outpouring of love. For example, someone may request prayer for a child who is seriously ill. Compassion wells up within our hearts, and we feel empathy for the individual as we place ourselves in his or her position. Hot tears flow down our cheeks as we pray earnestly. We can feel the love emanating from our souls. Our intercession in this situation is a labor of love.

When Jacob labored for Rachel, he worked for seven years and then seven more years without complaining or murmuring. "And Jacob served seven years for Rachel; and they seemed unto him but a few days, for the love he had to her" (Genesis 29:20). His work was a true labor of love.

A great way to express our love for those dear to us is by intercessory prayer. Face to face, at times it may be difficult to express fully our love and appreciation for others. Words often seem inadequate to reveal our feelings. Our sincere efforts to express our love seem to fall short at times, for the other person cannot see into our heart. But in prayer we can let love pour out for our family, fellow believers, and even enemies. God will understand, for He knows the intents of the heart.

Through intercession we can give our love to anyone we choose. Prayer is a manifestation and expression of love that no one can block. We can surround even those who hate us with love by our intercession.

How many times have we told people that we would pray for them and then either forgot to pray at all or just casually brought their names before the Lord? Usually we pray earnestly for those we truly love. Let us strive always to pray earnestly and sincerely.

Love means giving and sharing. True love is demonstrated and exemplified by giving to others. "For God so loved the world, that he gave his only begotten Son, that whosoever believeth in him should not perish, but have everlasting life" (John 3:16). "Husbands, love your wives, even as Christ also loved the church, and gave himself for it'' (Ephesians 5:25).

Jesus, our supreme example, lived His life entirely for others. He lived as a servant (Philippians 2:7). All through His life He constantly gave of Himself for others. He spent His life for others, pouring it out, not holding anything in reserve.

After preaching, teaching, healing the sick and comforting the downtrodden, He would still reach out to another person who needed to be helped. After living for others and giving of Himself, He gave His back to the lictor, His brow to the crown of thorns, and His hands and feet to the nails. He then gave His all, His precious blood and life itself.

He did not do it grudgingly or merely from a sense of debt and duty. For the joy of the end result He did it (Hebrews 12:2). The life, ministry, and atoning sacrifice of Jesus Christ was definitely a labor of love from the very heart and soul of God to us.

David's mighty men heard him thinking aloud as he reminisced one night in camp of his youthful years at home. They heard him talk about the water from the well at Bethlehem and how he would like to drink again from that well. Several of his men whose hearts were touched by this heartfelt expression began to make their way carefully through the darkness and the enemy lines to reach Bethlehem. They risked their lives, going through enemy territory to bring David the water from his boyhood well. He was so overcome with this expression of love that he poured the water out as an offering to the Lord. In deciding that he could not drink this water he said, ''Be it far from me, O LORD, that I should do this: is not this the blood of the men that went in jeopardy of their lives?" (II Samuel 23:17).

When giving comes from the heart, it is accomplished cheerfully and freely. Giving merely from a sense of duty does not provide the joy and satisfaction that comes when we pour ourselves out for the needs of others. II Corinthians 9:7 describes the proper attitude in giving: "Every man according as he purposeth in his heart, so let him give; not grudgingly, or of necessity: for God loveth a cheerful giver."

It is more blessed to give than it is to receive (Acts 20:35). Jesus instructed us, "Freely ye have received, freely give" (Matthew 10:8).

The attitude of the good Samaritan should be ours also in the realm of intercessory prayer. When he saw the bruised and beaten man lying by the side of the road, his heart was touched; he had compassion. Likewise compassion and empathy are vital to intercessory prayer. But he went beyond merely feeling sorry for the hapless victim and became involved. He could have dismissed the whole situation with reasoning such as "I am a hated Samaritan; why should I get involved?" But he got involved. He got blood and dirt on himself as he got down by the side of the victim. He was totally unselfish, as he was not going to gain anything from this experience except for the inward satisfaction of helping another. He also sacrificed, for he walked as the victim rode and he used money of his own to pay for a room at the inn. A labor of love will cause us to be involved, to sacrifice, to give for love's sake alone.

Intercessory prayer is a tremendous opportunity for giving, serving, and loving. Even the pauper can give in this area of service. Through intercessory prayer a person can pour out his soul and his love as he asks God to bless others.

We can pray for others' salvation without any reticence or reluctance. If we desire to see someone saved, healed, or blessed in a certain area, we can unabashedly tell the Lord all about it. We should let this prayer be a labor of love, and let it flow from within.

Colossians 4:12 speaks of intercessory prayer as fervent labor. At times, we will labor and toil in prayer. Sometimes when we pray it seems that we have direct and immediate access to heaven. At such times, we feel that we could ask God for anything as we bask in the Holy of Holies. At other times our praying is more strenuous and labored. Many times this is due to a spiritual battle. If we have searched our heart and have no condemnation, it is likely that we are facing spiritual opposition from the adversary. It is not a time to retreat or become fainthearted, however; rather it is time for faith, determination, and perseverance. It is the time to press onward, to labor in prayer. Truly in such an hour our intercession is a labor of love.

In 1972 when my father was terminally ill I had such an experience. I talked with him on the telephone, and he was in great pain and agony. I went over to the church one morning by myself and began to seek God for my father. For some reason I went into a Sunday school classroom, got down on the floor, and became very intense in intercessory prayer. I told the Lord that I was going to be submissive to His will as to whether Dad was healed or not. But I wanted the Lord to relieve the severe pain that he was experiencing. The Lord and I had a lengthy conversation, and it was a labor of love that compelled me that morning. I poured out the love in my heart and expected God to move. I talked with Dad shortly afterwards and he told me, "Son, I don't know what happened, but the pain is gone." What an opportunity and privilege that we have to express our love for those we are burdened for by the vehicle of intercession!

At times while we are in prayer, an individual or family may come to our minds as we meditate upon the Lord. We can then take them to the Lord and ask God to meet their needs. A missionary who is on the back shelf of our memory will suddenly step onto the center stage of our mind, and we can pray earnestly for him. Though he does not know that we are praying for him, the love of God in our hearts for him is poured out freely, and ten thousand miles away he feels the effects of our labor of love.

Along with my pastorate, I tune pianos for a living. After having tuned many thousands of pianos I have noticed that the best tuners are those who have a love and appreciation for the instrument. Those who tune just to make money and run to the next appointment seem to struggle with the pianos to get them tuned. But the experienced tuner who has an affection for the piano can seemingly coax the best out of the piano. The piano is just wood and metal, an inanimate musical instrument, but the tuner who understands the idiosyncrasies of the instrument will be patient in bringing out the best that the instrument is capable of. Often it is a labor of love to bring out the rich harmonics. Many times it is sheer toiling and laborious work.

Paul was an intense man, one who lived wholeheartedly. He gave his all to the work of God, withholding nothing for himself. He labored in prayer. He described his intercession for the Galatians by saying, "My little children, of whom I travail in birth again until Christ be formed in you" (Galatians 4:19). He labored physically and spiritually. "For ye remember, brethren, our labour and travail" (I Thessalonians 2:9).

Early in the history of the church the apostles decided, "We will give ourselves continually to prayer, and to the ministry of the word" (Acts 6:4). They had seen Jesus, the Great Intercessor, in action and they desired to emulate Him. Jesus had prayed for them, and they had been affected by His praying. They had asked Him, "Teach us to pray." And now at the helm of the young church, they recognized the importance and necessity of prayer. They wanted to give themselves to it.

Today the church is in the final reaping of this age. The Lord is still looking for laborers who will labor in prayer along with the other necessary avenues of service. But it is vital that we be compelled and constrained by love and not duty alone.

Chapter Seven

For Whom Should We Intercede?

In order to make our prayers most effective, it is important to be specific, and in this regard a prayer list is very helpful. It does not hinder the spirit of prayer to open one's eyes from time to time and look at a list of people to pray for. Using a prayer list is a good way not to omit people that we need to take to the throne of God in prayer. Such a list also helps us to focus our prayer for individuals.

Sometimes we may pray in a general way, such as, "Lord, bless the home missionaries today," or "Lord, protect your pastors as they minister in their respective cities." Any prayer is good, but focused prayer is more effective.

A shotgun scatters its birdshot over a wide area leaving many holes in the pattern. A rifle sends one projectile but with greater force. Laser beams are powerful because they focus a beam of light on a specific point. A focused laser beam is now able to remove plaque from certain arteries. In the spiritual realm, focused praying is more powerful and productive.

It is helpful to keep a prayer list in a diary or record book and to record when prayers are answered. A prayer list can be kept near the kitchen sink so a person can pray while doing dishes, or it can be kept in other places where it will serve as a reminder. If a prayer list is used in an automobile, it needs to be short and used prudently so as not to have an accident. In one's Bible is a good place to keep a prayer list, so that it is handy for prayer before and after church services.

On some days we have more time to pray than on others. A brief prayer list can be used on days when time is limited, and a more lengthy prayer list can be used when there is more time to pray.

Who should be on the prayer list? There are scriptural admonitions regarding whom we should pray for, and there are other obvious needs that we will mention in this chapter.

The Foreign Missions Division of the United Pentecostal Church has a group of volunteers called the Prayer Band Partners. They pray for the needs of the foreign missionaries and the Foreign Missions Division. They would be most grateful for any new additions.

The Harvestime radio broadcast, which beams the saving gospel message around the world, has a Harvestime Prayer Band. Volunteers are needed to pray that the messages preached on the radio will touch lives.

The local church may have a prayer request box where prayer requests are deposited. These can be added to the prayer list. Though we may not know the details about each request in the box, we can pray for them.

As we pray, the Lord will bring other people to mind so that we will pray for them. Often when I am in prayer the Lord will bring people and needs to my mind so that I can pray for them. As soon as I have prayed for one, another one comes to my mind. And on it will go until sometimes I will go through a whole list of people that the Lord laid on my heart. Sometimes I can see them in my imagination as I pray for them.

Recently while I was praying, the Lord burdened my heart for a certain pastor who is a friend of mine. He lives a long way from me in a cold and snowy part of the country. His name dropped before me even though I had not been thinking of him at all recently. I prayed for him and later tried to contact him. When I was finally able to reach him, I told him of my burden to pray for him. He told me that several weeks previously he was driving in snow following a snow plow when the throttle stuck on his truck. He had to make a decision whether to hit the snow plow or the snow bank. He headed into the snow bank and God spared him. We did not have a way to check the dates, but it is possible that God burdened me to pray for him because his life was in danger.

This incident illustrates the importance of listening to God. All the glory belongs to God, for He gave the burden and He performed the work. If God gives us the name of someone in prayer, we should pray for that person, for our intercession may be instrumental in saving that person's life or soul.

Current events can add requests to our prayer list. When a severe storm swept through America recently, depositing ice and snow across much of the country, I felt led to pray that God's people would be protected. When a hurricane was supposed to hit the coast of Texas recently, our church prayed earnestly for God's people in the path of the storm. These are just two examples of how we can be used of God in intercession by praying concerning daily events.

We should pray for government leaders and officials. The Bible tells us to pray for those in authority in government positions. (See I Timothy 2:1-2.) God is using North America to help propagate the gospel by sending missionaries. At the same time a floodtide of wickedness and immorality is sweeping across the land. Let us pray so we can have a little longer to do the work of God. Decisions in courts, legislatures, and executive offices affect us greatly as to our religious freedom and moral principles. We have a keen responsibility to pray for those in government positions, whether in federal, state, provincial, or local offices.

We should pray for our organizational leaders. God has blessed the United Pentecostal Church over the years, and we have been able to send out the light of this glorious gospel by means of foreign missionaries, home missionaries, radio broadcasts, and other avenues of outreach. We have been blessed with elected and appointed officials through the years who have helped us maintain doctrinal purity, a lifestyle of holiness, and a strong missions outreach. We should pray for our brethren in these positions at the general, district, and sectional levels.

We should pray for our foreign and home missionaries. These brave soldiers of the gospel are on the front lines of the spiritual offense. Let us not forget these faithful ones. Many home and foreign missionaries have greatly sacrificed and jeopardized their health for the sake of raising up a new work. I have seen some come close to the breaking point as they fought evil forces that resisted the truth being proclaimed where previously there was no witness. A foreign missionary recently told me that he did not realize the pressure that he lived under constantly until he was back in America for a few weeks and could sense the political freedom. He never knows from one day to the next concerning his adopted nation's political situation. Let us make sure that we include the missionaries on our prayer lists.

We should pray for our pastors and other ministers. Hebrews 13:17 says, "Obey them that have the rule over you, and submit yourselves: for they watch for your souls." It is a heavy responsibility to be a pastor. He feels very keenly the weight of leadership of the people who look to him for guidance. The people who sit before him week after week depend upon him to care for them, direct them, and help them make heaven. Very near the top of a person's prayer list should be the name of the pastor and his wife. They are important people in each person's life.

We should pray for one another. James 5:16 tells us to do so. As members of the body of Christ we must hold each other up in prayer. No one lives or dies to himself (Romans 14:7). God did not intend for us to be hermits or loners. He intends for us to function as an integrated, unified body of people. (See I Corinthians 12.) Thus what affects one person will ultimately affect others. We must pray for each other.

And we can each add to this list various other categories in our own lives. We should intercede for loved ones who are unsaved; visitors in our church services; backsliders; the youth of the church, who face a different set of temptations than years ago; people who are being taught home Bible studies; bus ministries and other outreach arms of the local church; neighbors and work associates; elderly shut-ins who do not get to attend services often; and members of our immediate family. There are many for us to pray for.

During the course of a day we can pray many small prayers for people as they come to our mind. This is one way we can pray without ceasing. For example, if someone's face pops into our mind, we can whisper a brief prayer for him as we go on our way. This type of prayer should not replace our normal prayer time but can be in addition to our regular praying.

As we go through our prayer list, it is good to mingle praise, thanksgiving, and worship with petitions and intercession.

Even though it is helpful to use a prayer list in order to be more thorough and complete, we must not let it make our prayer formal and ritualistic. We must not be set in concrete, but we need to follow the leading of the Spirit of God. For example, part way through the prayer list, the Lord may stop us right there and lead us to devote the remainder of our prayer time largely to one individual. We may not always get to cover all the names on our prayer list. But the list is a systematic way of making sure we include certain people in our usual prayers.

We need to take time in prayer. Many people are in a hurry and rush through their prayer time, but we should savor the moments in the sweet presence of the Lord, basking in and enjoying the fellowship of the Spirit. As we wait upon the Lord, He may bring people to our mind to intercede for.

Sometimes the Lord lays a burden upon our hearts to pray for another person. The next chapter explains, how we can be used of God in this manner.

Chapter Eight

The Prayer Burden

When we hear the word *burden,* we may think of a woman in a foreign land carrying a large load on her head. Or we may think of a beast carrying a heavy load on its back as it trudges wearily along.

In our discussion we will use the word to describe a deep concern for someone in need, or a weight that settles over our heart and draws us to pray to find release.

Not all prayer burdens have the same impact upon us. Some of them move us to prayer but we still carry on our normal routine of life otherwise. Other burdens are so strong and heavy that they affect us greatly, causing us to weep and mourn or to cancel some activities in order to give ourselves to prayer. Some prayer burdens take a toll on us physically for a time.

It is important to govern the burden and not allow it to ruin our health. But neither should we treat it lightheartedly and shrug it off. God depends upon us to pray regarding that burden.

Brother Billy Cole stated that his wife carried a heavy

burden for the lost and gave herself to deep intercession for three to four hours daily in a certain country. Consequently her health broke and she was seriously ill for a while.

A person must govern his burden. This is not to say that we should be casual about it, but we should be sensible and use wisdom. We are not physically capable of carrying the entire world on our shoulders.

It is very important to be sensitive to the Holy Spirit and learn to recognize a prayer burden. It can manifest itself as a feeling of apprehension or impending danger for someone. God may impart a feeling of urgency so that we will pray immediately. Someone's name may come to mind without any forethought at all. At times a burden can seem almost like a physical ailment such as a heavy feeling in the pit of the stomach. If it is a burden for a lost soul, we may actually feel a little taste of God's sorrow. We must not confuse a burden with a physical health problem. A spiritually sensitive individual will learn to recognize a prayer burden.

A prayer burden comes from God. In certain cases God may deal with people about their own needs. If they are lukewarm or backslidden God may deal with them to repent and pray for themselves. In such a case, the person needs to search his heart.

But in most situations, the burden is for someone else. God always looks for volunteers who will make themselves available to minister in intercessory prayer. Thus He gives prayer burdens to saints who are living overcoming lives and who desire to be used of God in intercession for others.

A burden can also come from other people as they

make us aware of needs and we feel concern for these situations.

In the Bible Nehemiah, the king's cupbearer, received a visit from friends who described the deplorable condition of Jerusalem. He was extremely moved by their report. He was so moved with compassion and concern that his countenance was affected. He could not conceal his grief. In his case, the source of the burden was his friends, and God also moved upon him.

God may give us a prayer burden because a crisis is happening at that moment and He wants us to pray right then. At other times danger may be imminent and God burdens us to pray before it occurs.

Recently Brother Richard Lee, a pastor in Flagstaff, Arizona, was driving in inclement weather from Phoenix to Flagstaff. Snow made the driving treacherous. At just a few minutes after ten o'clock at night he lost control of his pickup truck, hit a guard rail, and slid off the road. At the same time, a lady in the church felt a burden of prayer for Brother and Sister Lee. God protected them and they were unhurt.

The Lord works through the members of His body to give them a prayer burden at times when another member is in need. God trusts us to be obedient and pray at such times. He has sensitive, godly people who have prayed many times and helped avert many a crisis, known and unknown.

Timing is of the utmost importance when we receive a prayer burden. We must pray at once. We must give it priority over other activities, for it may be a life-and-death situation. We must be willing to pray whether it be for a few minutes or if necessary for hours until the burden is released.

One saint received a prayer burden and told the Lord that she would pray in a few minutes. He impressed her with the thought, "You must pray now! If you don't pray now, he will die." She did not know whom the burden was for, but a missionary's son was lying close to death at that very moment and needed a touch from God. She dropped everything and prayed right then. A miracle took place, and the missionary's son was spared.

A prayer burden may or may not come at a convenient hour. If it is not an emergency situation, God may give a prayer burden at our regular time of prayer. If it is an emergency, the Lord may call upon someone in the middle of the night or in the middle of the family dinner time.

When God gives us a prayer burden, He intends for us to do something about it. God can do His work without our help, for He is omnipotent. But He chooses to work through us many times and involve members of His church in meeting the needs of others. We are blessed by giving of our love and care, and others become recipients of divine providence as well as our love.

When people participate in intercession, they are truly an asset to the kingdom of God. Instead of hiding their talents in the earth, they use themselves for the work of God. And there is great personal fulfillment and joy in being used of the Lord to help others who are in need.

A church may experience a prayer burden in the middle of a worship service. Sometimes the pastor will feel it and convey his feelings to the congregation. The Spirit of the Lord will confirm it as a weeping spirit and a heaviness comes upon the church.

One Sunday night a prayer burden came upon me as I led the service in our local assembly. I told the congregation that I felt led for us to pray for a certain missionary. I felt a strong pull on me and I conveyed this to our church. The people began to weep, and the Lord moved upon us as we interceded. I saw the missionary at the general conference shortly thereafter. As I shared with him what had transpired in our service, tears welled up in his eyes and he said to me, "You were right on target." He had been under heavy pressure and attack and needed our prayers.

While I was a pastor on the East Coast our church experienced a prayer burden one Sunday night that was so strong it affected the entire service. As service time came and we began to worship in praise and singing, a heaviness and weeping swept over the congregation in a mighty wave. It was impossible to have what we would call a normal service. Without any of us having any knowledge of it, a short time before a family from our church was involved in a severe automobile accident. Their car was hit from the rear by a car driven at a high rate of speed. The collision catapulted their car, and their hatchback came open, ejecting three of the four family members onto the side of the road. Their lives were spared by a miracle of God. God had directed us as members of the church to pray with a spirit of intercession. When the burden of prayer came over us, the accident had already happened, but the Lord led us to pray about the time they went to the hospital for treatment and then were taken home.

Sometimes we know whom we are burdened for, and other times we will have a burden of prayer for persons unknown.

The intensity of our prayer burden often depends upon the immensity of the situation. If the need is great, involving many souls or a servant of the Lord who is in great danger, the burden may be very intense. The intensity of the burden may also be affected by how immediately action is needed. In the case of Brother and Sister Lee of Flagstaff, they needed prayer immediately, as their motor vehicle was in an accident at the time the Lord burdened the lady from their church.

Recently I was tuning a piano one afternoon near Mesa, Arizona, when a tremendous heaviness came over me. I did not recognize at first what was happening. I had just finished eating lunch, and I thought I was possibly getting ill from some bad food. And then I observed that I was in the home of a Mormon family and thought that possibly I was feeling satanic forces. I finished the piano and walked out to my vehicle actually staggering somewhat. When I began to drive away, the Lord helped me to understand that the heaviness was an intense prayer burden.

I drove down the road toward town travailing, moaning and groaning in prayer. I knew that someone was in great need somewhere. It was long distance to my home, but I thought that I needed to contact my home in case something was wrong there. I did not call but continued on praying in the Spirit.

The prayer burden lasted for perhaps thirty to forty minutes when suddenly and instantly it left. A tremendous release and joy followed. I began to weep and rejoice profusely. I was near the edge of town, so I parked my vehicle, walked out into the desert for a short distance, and continued worshiping the Lord for a while. To this day I do not know whom I was praying for, but there was no mistaking the heavy weight of the prayer burden on my soul.

A prayer burden should not be confused with anxiety or undue worry. Anxiety and worry come about by our concern over a situation and by our failure to place it in the hands of the Lord. Fretting, frustration, and worry over a situation are not a prayer burden. These emotions originate from within us as we feel threatened or helpless.

A prayer burden comes from the Lord when He wants us to intercede in prayer for someone or a situation. We pray until we feel that the burden is released, and then we offer praise and worship to God for answering the prayer. We should pray until we "pray through," feeling release from the burden. A feeling of joy and peace comes at such a time. We should not simply live with a prayer burden and not pray. The burden comes to us so we will pray concerning it.

A burden may be for a particular city, country, or continent. It may be a perpetual burden that we have for many months. Each time it comes upon us, we should pray until release comes. Perhaps the next day or week it will return, and we pray for it again.

A pastor may have a similar burden for his city or community. Each time he prays with a burdened heart for his field of labor, he prays until he gets release. But quite often, perhaps daily, he prays again with a burdened heart for his town. It is a perpetual burden that he lives with.

Most churches have some mature, stable saints who in a sense share the same burden for their town as the pastor. Though they may not feel the weight as heavy as the pastor since he has the call of God to that city, they feel a measure of the same burden as he does. These faithful saints are to a great degree responsible for the revivals that many churches experience. Such a prayer burden can mean feeling God's sorrow over the lost souls in the city and His compassion for them. Jesus wept over Jerusalem, and He wants us to weep with concerned and burdened hearts for the lost where we are.

A prayer burden may be for a one-time situation where a crisis has arisen. We feel it, pray concerning it, and feel it lift. After a period of time, God may use us again for another situation or emergency.

We must be sensitive to the voice of the Lord to recognize a prayer burden and act upon it when it comes. What an opportunity it is to be used of the Lord to bless others!

In order for our intercession to be effective, we must have faith in God. (See Hebrews 11:6; James 1:6-7.) For any prayer to be effective, we must believe God. When He gives us a prayer burden, we must pray with faith and place it in His hands. Faith and trust in God will help us to pray until we have release and victory.

There may be occasions when we feel the liberty to call a prayer partner and ask that person to unite in prayer with us over the prayer burden. In other situations we may feel that we should not tell anyone else but simply pray ourselves.

Chapter Nine

The Sensitive Soul

*I*n the natural realm some people fail to see the beauty of the more obscure, simple things in this world. They overlook the kaleidoscope of color in a group of fallen leaves lying in a pool of clear water as the autumn sun shines upon them. The Grand Canyon may be awesome to them in its size but its beauty may escape them as the rays of light cast shadows across the mesas and ravines. They may miss the subtle changes that mark the progression of the seasons or the smell of a spring morning after an April shower. They may overlook the sparkle of love in the countenance of a June bride or the light in a child's eyes.

Others are more sensitive and given to introspection. When they hear a symphony, the slightest nuances of sound do not escape them. They sense the beauty in things others overlook such as a butterfly or the afternoon panorama of God's brush strokes of color as He paints an Arizona sunset. They sense by changes in expression the feelings and emotions of their loved ones. We say they are sensitive people.

It is the same in the spiritual realm. Some people, like Elijah, hear the thunder, feel the earthquake, and see the fire. Some wait for God to speak in an audible voice or in a loud, boisterous way to get their attention. They want God to thunder from heaven or send an angel to give them instructions. God can do any of these things if He chooses, but He usually speaks to us differently.

After the wind, earthquake, and fire, a still, small voice came to Elijah by which he received instructions from the Lord (I Kings 19:12-18). In normal situations God usually speaks to us through His written Word, the mouth of a preacher as he preaches, or in the still, small voice of gentle impressions on the mind.

The spiritually sensitive children of God do not have to hear thunder from God, but the soft, tender voice of the Lord speaks loudly and unmistakably to them. They exercise their "spiritual radar" enough to recognize when God speaks to them as opposed to their flesh or the enemy. Of course, we should test a message by the Word of God to determine whether it is from God.

In such an important area of the work of God as intercession, we must develop a sensitivity to God's voice. When God speaks with soft, gentle impressions, calling us to pray, we do not want to fail the Lord. This chapter offers some suggestions and guidelines for developing spiritual sensitivity.

Spiritual sensitivity does not mean wearing our feelings on our sleeves or having a chip on our shoulder. Some people are so hypersensitive that a person is afraid to say anything to them for fear of offending them. Such people are spiritually immature. In contrast, spiritual sensitivity means praying, seeking God, and being quick to respond to the voice of God. Through experience such people develop a tenderness toward the voice of God. They learn how to recognize the Lord talking when others may not.

In my work as a piano tuner a sensitive, trained ear is essential. One of the adjustments that I make on a fairly regular basis is called "voicing" the hammers that strike the strings, which involves needling with a set of needles the wool hammers to change the tone of the instrument. In order to accomplish this, the surroundings must be quiet so that I can hear the slightest change in tone coloration. Anyone could hear the same thing that I hear except that their ears are not trained to discern the sound. Likewise, the sensitive child of God does not need the Lord to talk loudly, for he has learned to discern the "whisper" of the tender voice of God calling him to prayer.

Here are some suggestions for developing sensitivity to the voice of the Lord.

Allow time after prayer to wait upon the Lord. There are so many demands for our time that it requires real discipline to wait regularly upon the Lord. After we have finished talking to the Lord, He can direct us to pray for certain people or specific needs if we will wait upon Him. Our carnal minds tell us that important things need our attention, but waiting upon God is important also.

Allow time each day for solitude and reflection. It can be just a fifteen-minute quiet time when we shut out the cares of the day and its problems. We can take a walk or put a gospel tape in the stereo and allow God to speak to us. It helps to get away from the telephone and the desk. At such times God often gives names of people to add to our prayer list or impresses us with a prayer burden.

Learn not to be preoccupied with personal cares and problems always. I like to devote a portion of my early morning to listening to the Lord and meditating. Invariably the enemy will try to distract me by things I must do that day. I try to push these things aside for a while to center my thoughts on the Lord. To train ourselves to be sensitive to the Lord's voice requires a real effort to bring our minds into captivity.

Look for the subtle ways that God may be speaking. The Lord may seek our attention by impressing a passage of Scripture upon our minds or using a gospel song. People who cross our paths during the day may not only need help or a witness, but the Lord may want us to add them to our prayer list.

Take advantage of opportunities in the daily schedule to listen. If a person rides the bus to work, he may have thirty minutes to meditate. He can close his eyes for a few moments and enter into his prayer closet to pray quietly. Another person may have a few minutes in the morning at his desk before the business of the day begins. One man used part of his lunch hour every day for his personal study and devotions.

Listen as well as talk when you pray. Usually we talk a lot more than we listen when we pray. Let us develop the courtesy of giving God a fair amount of time to whisper in our ears. It is hard to hear when we are always talking.

Do not harden your heart against the voice of God. Hebrews 3:7-8 admonishes us not to harden our hearts but to hear the voice of God. It is possible to shrug off or push off the gentle entreaties of the Spirit of God and grieve Him. It is also possible to become calloused and indifferent to Him. We want to be tender and respond quickly when He speaks.

As Billy Cole has observed, when we are walking close to God and receive a first impression about a spiritual matter it is usually God speaking. Often a second impression, will quickly follow from the flesh or carnal mind, which tries to talk us out of what God has just spoken. Then a third impression may come from the devil, who also tells us that what we heard originally was not God.

Our carnal reasoning is an enemy of spiritual sensitivity. The negative spiritual input that the world bombards us with all day long also counteracts the voice of God.

We can harden our heart against the voice of God by the cares of life or by selfishness. Being overcharged with the cares of life or living in their own private world causes many people to close their ears to the gentle whisper of the Holy Ghost.

Learn from past experiences with God in prayer. In developing a sensitive spirit to the voice of God, we can draw from our past experiences to recognize when God talks to us. While we cannot live in the past, the past provides a good frame of reference in many situations. (See Romans 5:3-4.)

Use fasting as an aid in developing spiritual sensitivity. Fasting makes us more aware of the Spirit of God. When we fast with spiritual motivation the flesh becomes more dull and we become more responsive to God. We push aside the daily routine of eating and deliberately set our affections upon God. We make ourselves more available to hear from God. Food often makes us sluggish, while fasting works the opposite. Fasting will make a difference in spiritual sensitivity.

Keep the heart clean before God. To be sensitive to God, we must be in right relationship to Him. If our heart condemns us and guilt burdens us down, then we are in no condition to intercede for another until we first repent. (See I John 3:20-22.) We must be honest before God to be on good speaking terms with Him.

Be submissive to the pastor. God will not violate His principles of order in the church. God desires to use the various members of the body in intercessory prayer, but regardless of how much a person is used of God, he must remain submissive to spiritual leadership. Being sensitive to the Spirit of God and being used of God greatly do not qualify one to instruct the pastor in spiritual matters. If God uses a saint in unusual ways to intercede for others, he should still consult with his pastor and be submissive. The pastor of a church is a spiritually sensitive person himself and knows how to feel after God. He will appreciate the help that intercessors provide to the kingdom of God.

Stay humble as God uses you. There is a danger in becoming proud or arrogant when we are used of God in a great way. When we see how God answers our prayers and uses our lives to bless others, we can have a human tendency to think more of ourselves than we ought. We must not become self-righteous or lifted up in pride, but we must remain humble and always give God the glory for whatever is accomplished. We should desire to be used of God, but we should beware of the dangers lurking in our flesh.

Relax in the presence of the Lord. Prayer is foremost a relationship with someone who is very dear to us, the Lord Jesus Christ. We should not take the Lord for granted nor be irreverent or disrespectful. We should forever be in awe of Him. We are small, and He is great. Nevertheless, He has saved us by His grace and we are His children. We can be comfortable in His presence, for He is our heavenly Father. We cannot stand in His presence by our own merits, but He has redeemed us and made us worthy. When we have a proper concept of what God's grace has done, we can relax and enjoy His presence without guilt or condemnation.

God said, "Be still, and know that I am God" (Psalm 46:10). We do not have to work ourselves up into an emotional state of frenzy, although love is emotional and we often become emotional in worship. God often speaks after we rejoice, perhaps express ourselves demonstratively, and then become subdued and quiet. At that point we are often most sensitive to hear His still, small voice.

Learn to feel after God (Acts 17:27). Each prayer time is different just as each church service is a new experience. Just as we may shout in church one time and weep in the next service, so we should not get into a rut or become ritualistic in our prayer. Israel had to learn to be flexible and move when the cloud (presence of God) moved. Likewise, we must learn to feel after the Spirit when we pray. We need to flow with God so we can be in His will and hear from Him. We must hear from Him so we can receive direction for our intercession.

Chapter Ten

Prevailing Intercession

To prevail means to gain ascendancy through strength or superiority. It also means to become effectual or effective. Prevailing intercession is prayer that overcomes obstacles and is effective.

Knowing how to prevail in prayer is important because the hour is late and time is running out on this world. We must redeem the time and pray effectively. The stakes are high. Lost souls hang in the balance.

We can experience victory in prayer. Opposition to our intercession comes from our flesh and from Satan and his forces. Weak, faint-hearted Christians will not be victorious in prayer, for prevailing intercession requires diligent effort. Many never experience victory because when they come up against opposition they do not persevere. But when we persist in intercession, no barrier that the enemy erects can block our prayers forever, for the gates of hell shall not prevail against the church (Matthew 16:18).

We Must Prevail with God in Prayer

God desires to answer our prayers, but He wants us to be earnest. He will not answer every little whim we have, but He wants to see how sincere we really are. God does not hold answers to prayer in His closed hand for us to pry out of His fingers. He waits to answer our petitions, but He sometimes waits for a period of time to test our sincerity and desire.

When a woman of Canaan asked Jesus to heal her daughter, He did not do so right away. At that time He was ministering primarily to the Israelites, and He told her that He was sent to the lost sheep of Israel. But she persisted in asking for His help. She humbled herself and worshiped Him even after she was rebuffed. Jesus was touched by her faith and delivered her daughter after testing her desire and faith.

Jacob prevailed with God in prayer and received what he desired. His name was changed and he never walked the same again. It took a great amount of desire and persistence for Jacob to prevail as long as he did. He would not let God go until He received a blessing.

Jesus told a parable concerning an unjust judge and a widow to teach the importance of persistence in prayer (Luke 18:1-8). He used an extreme example to bring out a scriptural truth: prevailing intercession is persistent praying.

James 5:16 says, "The effectual fervent prayer of a righteous man availeth much." Fervent means to exhibit a great intensity of feeling; to be hot, glowing, boiling, or zealous.

When an individual is so consumed by spiritual desire to see someone saved that his whole being is affected, then he is fervent in prayer. His voice inflection will probably display his emotions, and tears will probably flow down his cheeks as he intercedes urgently and fervently.

To prevail in intercessory prayer, one must have a burning desire. Those who are apathetic will never pursue prayer long enough to get very far. And if a person truly desires to see God move, he will persist in prayer because he really cares about the outcome. If the Lord places a prayer burden upon us for a lost soul or someone in need and we have enough desire, we will persist until we pray to victory. God does not like lukewarmness and apathy. Fiery, white-hot praying with burning desire moves the heart of God. This kind of prayer conquers, overcoming obstacles and prevailing.

When an individual is full of zeal and living victoriously, he will have a burden for the lost and for others. That burden will become a desire that propels him to intercessory prayer. And if that desire is fanned by the fires of God, it will become fervent and white hot, and the person will prevail with God in intercession.

Let us keep fanning and refueling the fire, for intercessors are needed. It is not time for timid, reticent, apathetic attitudes but time to be fervent and on fire in the prayer rooms.

Prevailing intercession is praying with the whole heart (Jeremiah 29:12-14). It involves the entire being. It can make a person physically weak, weary, and exhausted. At times prayer is joyful and blissful; at other times it is agonizingly hard work. It resembles a physical wrestling match at times as we are involved in spiritual combat.

Epaphras labored fervently in prayer for others (Colossians 4:12). When Moses and David prayed for Israel, they were emotionally involved and fervent in intercession. They labored and agonized with their whole heart, and they prevailed in prayer as God answered them.

When I was a small boy, our family attended a church pastored by Brother J. C. Cole in Parkersburg, West Virginia. Brother and Sister Cole had a small daughter named Ruth who contracted leukemia. The church had many and lengthy prayer meetings for her. I can still remember how my parents were touched by her illness. When Dad went down to visit her, Ruth said to him, "Brother Holman, don't stop praying."

God is saying to His church today, "Intercessors, don't stop praying." The lost need our prayers, the church needs our prayers, and God depends upon us to intercede. He depends upon us to prevail with fervent desire and persistence.

To prevail with God necessitates praying in accordance with His Holy Word and in submission to His will. (See I John 5:14-15.) We know for a certainty that it is His will to save the lost (II Peter 3:9). And if He places a prayer burden upon us, He wants us to intercede. But if we initiate a request, we must pray in accordance with scriptural guidelines and the will of God.

We Must Prevail over the Flesh

The flesh is one of our greatest enemies in doing the will of God. We must subdue it and bring it under subjection to God. The flesh does not like to pray, for it constantly wars against the inner person. One reason our flesh does not want to pray is that it does not want to spend the time in prayer necessary to prevail.

"Microwave" prayers are okay for emergencies and at the dinner table. At times of emergency we may only have time for a brief prayer. But in order to have an effective prayer life we must take ample time to seek God.

Often the prayers recorded in the Bible seem quite brief. Elijah's prayer that brought fire down from heaven was short. But we can be sure that the prayer warriors mentioned in Scripture did considerable praying and built up a reservoir of spiritual power so that when they faced critical hours they could touch God quickly. In Gethsemane, Jesus prayed three hours in one-hour increments. The Bible also records that Jesus spent all night in prayer at times, and can the church do less?

Some spiritual battles seem to be won easily, but most of them are hard-fought, agonizing struggles. And they take time. Intercessory prayer is not for those with little resolve, for the enemy does not relinquish his hold on souls easily. We must be willing to take whatever time is needed to seek God and to break through for others in intercession.

We learn to pray by praying. Guidelines and instructions on prayer can educate and inspire us, but the best way to learn how to prevail in intercession is through experience. To improve our prayer life, we must practice prayer.

We do not spend time in prayer to earn favors or to work our way to heaven. But we crucify our flesh, disciplining it so that we can prevail in intercession.

In prevailing over our flesh, we must escape the prison of self and selfishness. Intercession is unselfish praying. Sometimes we must forget our own needs or place them down the list below the needs of others. We must break out of the selfish mentality of our day and develop a vision of the needs of others and the perishing multitudes.

To prevail in prayer requires humility on our part. If God uses us, we must remember to give God the glory. Without Him we are nothing and can do nothing. There is always a risk that when we are used of God we can become proud or haughty or take God's glory.

Recently, on a trip through northern California, I passed miles of vineyards. The pruning process had removed most of the branches, leaving the main vines looking bare. But I was told that in a few months new branches would grow and produce fruit. The branches were expendable, but the vine lived on. Likewise, Jesus is the vine and we are the branches. We are simply instruments in His hands and must remember to keep a spirit of humility. We can be removed. He, the source of life, has blessed us with life and the opportunity for service in His vineyard. And we can serve Him in many ways, including prayers of intercession.

To prevail over our flesh requires us to keep our hearts right in the sight of God. We must be honest and sincere. We must be free from guilt and condemnation. We must be forgiving and live a repentant, overcoming, holy life separated from the ways of the world. The world is full of negativism, but the intercessor lives in the realm of faith. Spiritual pollution everywhere seeks entrance into our mind and soul. Filthy conversation by co-workers on the job and ungodly magazines at the checkout line in the grocery store seek to pollute our thinking. To prevail in intercession requires us to keep our minds pure and focused on God. This requires real discipline on our part.

We Must Prevail over the Enemy

When we purpose in our heart to give ourselves to intercessory prayer, we will meet the enemy head on. Intercessory prayer takes souls out of his clutches, which means war. Intercession aids God's people when they are in trouble, while the enemy seeks to destroy them. Intercessory prayer is serious, for souls are at stake.

The enemy will try to bluff us as a roaring lion, and within our own strength we are no match for him. But we do not have to fear the devil. "Greater is he that is in you, than he that is in the world" (I John 4:4). The Lord is omnipotent and He resides within us. If we resist the devil he will flee (James 4:7).

The Lord who resides in our hearts has not left us defenseless or without offensive spiritual artillery. When we intercede for others we go on the offense. We do not have to sit passively on the sidelines watching souls go to hell without rising up in spiritual indignation. By intercession we can become prayer warriors in the heat of the battle on the front lines of combat.

Let us look at some of the weapons that we use in intercessory prayer to prevail over our enemy.

Faith is a weapon we use in prayer. "Fight the good fight of faith" (I Timothy 6:12). Faith is a creative force. Fear and unbelief are destructive forces. When we intercede, we should look ahead through eyes of faith and see the answer to our prayers. Our faith must not be in ourselves but in the power of God. The prayer of faith will rout the enemy. (See Matthew 21:21-22; James 1:6-8.)

A mighty weapon is the name of Jesus. We should go forward interceding under the banner of Jesus. "The name of the LORD is a strong tower: the righteous runneth into it, and is safe" (Proverbs 18:10). We have the authority to use that all-powerful name when we pray. (See John 14:14.) Demons cannot stand up against that name.

The written Word of God was the weapon used by Jesus on the mount of temptation. It is a powerful weapon to use when we claim the promises of God in intercessory prayer. I like to quote the Scriptures at times when I am involved in a spiritual conflict with the enemy. As we labor in prayer, we can prevail by quoting the promises of God, thereby taking up the sword of the Spirit, which is the Word of God (Ephesians 6:17).

A mighty weapon at our disposal is praying in the Spirit. In this dimension of prayer we cease to pray by our own direction and we follow the direction of the Holy Ghost, flowing with God. Often we will pray in tongues.

We can prevail over the enemy through praise and worship. When the battle is hot and we are pressing forward in prayer, we should take time to praise the Lord. Jehoshaphat found power in praise and worship when he faced the enemy (II Chronicles 20:21-22). Praise is a mighty weapon to prevail in prayer (Psalm 149:6-9).

The blood of Jesus has purchased our victory over sin and the devil. As redeemed children of God, we depend upon the atoning death, burial, and resurrection of Jesus as we resist the devil. "And they overcame him by the blood of the Lamb" (Revelation 12:11).

When we prevail in prayer until we break through the walls of resistance, it is easy to stop there, but that is the time when we can really be effective in prayer. That is the time to continue praying. When we rout the enemy and have clear access to the throne of God, we should continue with our intercession unhindered. In this way we can prevail and triumph in prayer.

Chapter Eleven

High-Intensity Intercession

The advertising world today uses terms such as "super," "giant size," "high performance" and other words to describe a product out of the ordinary. The automobile industry uses descriptions such as "turbo-charged," "high performance," and other adjectives to describe a vehicle that is brimming with power to spare.

Similarly, there is a dimension in prayer that goes beyond normal praying. When our intercession becomes directed by the Holy Ghost, our prayers become more focused and powerful. Ordinarily, using a prayer list and the various suggested ways of interceding for others is good and necessary. When we do not feel a particular burden for certain needs, people, or situations, a systematic method of prayer is excellent. But sometimes the Spirit of God directs and controls our prayers. This is praying in the Spirit, or what we can call high-intensity praying.

Praying in the Spirit may involve praying in tongues or it may mean flowing with the Holy Ghost as He directs our prayer as we speak in our native tongue. Often when we are praying in the Spirit we will speak in tongues at various times during our prayer. At other times we will feel a special unction of the Holy Ghost and pray in tongues for quite a length of time. (See Romans 8:26-27.)

One reason why high-intensity intercession is so effective and powerful is that we humans do not know the many needs and situations that God knows, and God can direct us to pray for requests that are the most pressing. God knows when there is an emergency somewhere, and He can direct us through His Spirit to pray for such needs. God may direct us to spend much of our prayer time on a particular situation or person.

Another reason for the effectiveness of this kind of prayer is that God's Spirit ensures that our prayers are in accordance with His will and in harmony with the proper solution to the problem. When we pray with our human reasoning, we may ask God to intervene in a certain way, but often we do not know what to ask Him to do about a situation. When God directs our intercession, He leads us to petition Him appropriately by giving us the words in tongues or otherwise impressing our minds to pray appropriately. When we pray in the Spirit we are more submissive to His will in our petitions.

It is important for us to let God speak to us regarding people to pray for. When names or faces of people flash before our minds in prayer, it may be God impressing us to pray for them. When the Holy Ghost flows and we are deep in prayer, God will often call names to our remembrance as fast as we pray for them. At times God calls to our mind people that we have not seen in years. We should not pass off these experiences lightly but be sensitive and obedient to God.

Several years ago a Samoan lady attended the church I pastored. Her knowledge of English was limited, and cultural differences made it difficult to communicate well with her. She had some difficulty in separating herself from certain worldly practices, and holiness of dress was new to her. One evening we were gathered around her at the altar in intercession, and she was having difficulty getting victory in prayer. Suddenly the Spirit of God came upon me with great force and power. I began to pray in tongues with a strong unction, and I felt that I was actually speaking to the lady. She burst out crying and began to say in English, "Yes, I will. Yes, I will." In a few moments she was filled with the Holy Spirit. A couple of days later, the lady who had brought her to church told me that she had been able to understand me when I was praying in tongues. I do not know whether I was speaking in Samoan or whether God helped her to interpret my prayer.

God through His Spirit can pray through us to accomplish things that we could not accomplish otherwise. When God directs our intercessory prayer, we can expect the supernatural and miraculous to take place.

Learning to pray is a lifelong pursuit. We will never fully arrive. I feel that I am in the elementary grades in learning about prayer. But if we will hunger and thirst after God in the prayer closet, He will use our lives as He directs us to pray in the Holy Ghost.

Since intercession is so vital to the cause of God, it is imperative that we involve ourselves in high-intensity intercession. When we pray in the Spirit, our faith soars as we have confidence that God is in control of our prayer and is leading us. And faith makes our prayers effective.

Without faith our prayers will not accomplish anything, but our faith reaches new heights in God when we pray in the Holy Ghost. As we ask God for the needs of others, a holy boldness comes over us and we have confidence that God will do whatever we ask of Him.

At times when God gives us a prayer burden, we will feel a strong direction of the Spirit to yield to God and pray in tongues. When God gives us a burden and directs our prayer, whether in other tongues or our native tongue, we can definitely expect results and answers.

At times a burden will intensify until a spirit of travail comes. This is a deep, intense form of intercession. Often when we pray in the Spirit our prayers become more intense and the weight of the burden increases until we groan and moan in the Spirit. Travail is not instituted or set in motion by us, but it is a deep burden that comes from God. Many never experience this type of prayer because they do not develop their prayer life to yield to God in this measure. Others do not want to experience this form of praying because it is so physically demanding.

The weight of Jesus' burden and travail was so heavy that His sweat was as great drops of blood. That is how intense His prayer was in Gethsemane (Luke 22:44).

Travailing prayer is powerful, and the results can be staggering. Enormous mountains of opposition and circumstances have been moved by this kind of praying.

When there are critical needs or life-and-death situations, it is time for the spiritual big guns. It is time to pray in the Spirit, and if God should so direct, to yield to Him in the spirit of travail. Then the gates of hell will tremble as prayer bombards the fortress of the enemy.

Brother Patrick Jinks, a minister from Tempe, Arizona, had an experience in which God used him in a spirit of travail to intercede for his family. Here is his account:

"Without a real knowledge of the word *travail* as it relates to prayer, I began praying one night for my parents. I prayed as I drove home late one night from church. The genuine loneliness added to the experience I was about to endure, as I drove for thirty minutes down long, winding, dark country roads. I prayed earnestly for my parents. I thought I was really standing in the gap, really interceding. The prayer was simple: 'Lord, save my mom and dad.'

"It did not stay that simple though. Suddenly I began to weep. First, it was out of grief, as though someone I loved was dying. But then I began to see and feel things in the Spirit that I had never seen or felt. I could see through my parents' eyes. I started to feel the weight on their shoulders. I understood their trials, their physical sufferings, their fear, their frustrations, and their loneliness!

"Now I was not grieving for myself because I had lost something, but I grieved for them because of what they were experiencing in life without the Lord. My weeping soon turned to sobbing. I found myself crying with a loud voice and not even saying words anymore—just sobbing. I couldn't stop. It was actually hard to breathe. I was not enjoying this prayer. In fact, I wanted to stop, but I could not.

"Finally, I was able to gain control of my prayer again. Now I understand that it was not just my prayer. It was the prayer of my parents. It was what they would have cried out for if they had possessed the spiritual sensitivity to do so. Since they did not, I stepped in. I literally took the burden to God for them. Today my parents are full of the Holy Ghost and faithfully involved in God's church. Now I understand why Jesus Himself became a man to take on our pain and our burdens and relieve them at the cross.

"I felt all their needs, and it did not feel good. It was not an enjoyable experience. But the fruit was worth the labor. It was a small price to pay to have the privilege of contributing to the work of the kingdom of God and to learn the value and meaning of intercessory prayer."

The times in which we live call for desperate people and desperate action—not desperate in the sense of surrendering to the overwhelming powers of darkness but desperate to the point of getting ahold of God in a greater dimension of prayer. Much could be said of the plight of souls and nations of the world. The task before us at times seems to overwhelm us. In our own strength we do not have hope, but through Christ we can do all things. And it is time to reach for the depths in prayer to conquer for God. It is time for high-intensity intercession for the needs of the world today. We need to know how to pray in the Holy Spirit and how to yield to God in travailing prayer.

James 5:17 tells us that Elijah was an ordinary man who served an extraordinary God and prayed extraordinary prayers. The apostles who prayed until the place where they were assembled was shaken were people of flesh and blood who were filled with the same Holy Spirit that we possess. Today God still uses ordinary people like us who will pray in the Holy Spirit and with faith in God.

Chapter Twelve

The Intercessor and Personal Renewal

Intercession consists of unselfish praying. It means pouring out ourselves for the needs of another. It exacts a heavy toll on our physical body as we wring ourselves out in prayer. There is no way to avoid the strain, for we must pray with emotion and empathy. If we do not become emotionally involved in our praying, we probably do not have our heart and soul into it.

A prominent minister once stated that there was no way to become deeply involved in intercession and be effective without its leaving an effect physically. If we move in the realm of intercessory prayer, especially travailing and prevailing intercession, it will leave an imprint. Some people have become seriously ill, even to the point of death, because of intense intercession.

One reason why intercession can be so physically draining is that compassion and empathy pull love from within us to give to another. When our prayer is a labor of love, it can leave us very weak afterwards. Moreover, when we battle evil spirits in prayer, the spiritual warfare can take its toll on our physical bodies.

A strong prayer burden can nearly bowl a person over in its intensity. I have been under a prayer burden that was so heavy I groaned under its intensity until I was nauseated and fatigued.

We should not pamper our flesh or shrink back from being used of God in intercession, but we can learn to govern the intensity of a burden in order to be wise stewards of the life and health that God has given us. Of course, we should not quench the Spirit of God or grieve Him. And under the weight of a prayer burden, the very nature of the intercessor is to be unselfish and disregard his own welfare. Nevertheless, we need to take proper care for ourselves physically, mentally, and spiritually.

Romans 12:1 instructs us to present our bodies as a living sacrifice to God. And when we pour our hearts out in intercession we present our bodies a living sacrifice. But Romans 12:1 also talks about "reasonable service." God is reasonable and understands our physical limitations. Most of the time the problem is getting people to intercede at all, and many know nothing about deep intercession. But for those who desire to be used of God in a greater measure in intercession, it is important to use wisdom and discretion for health's sake. We are not a machine but a physical body of flesh, blood, and bones that has limitations.

Jesus Himself rested physically (Mark 4:38). And He advised His disciples that they should rest (Mark 6:31).

For health's sake, we should attempt to govern our burden. We do not need to be overly concerned and quench the Spirit of God by pampering the flesh, but we need to use wisdom.

Nature teaches us lessons of renewal. There is a cycle in life of giving and receiving. Old leaves fall and new ones grow the next spring. The snake sheds his skin and grows a new one. Birds moult and grow new plumage. The ground yields its moisture to the sun and clouds and receives it back again in the form of rain. Plants and animals freely give and receive for the benefit of other living things.

Intercession is the giving of our love, prayers, and concern for others. It is the opposite of prayers that are strictly for self and personal benefit. But in giving of ourselves, we must also learn to be a recipient or we will run dry and have nothing to give. We must be renewed.

After great spiritual victories and effort, there is often a physical letdown. The victor is often drained, exhausted, and weary. After Elijah experienced an exhilarating victory on Mount Carmel and a lengthy, powerful prayer meeting that brought earthly rain, he was weary, exhausted, and discouraged (I Kings 19). He needed physical and emotional renewal. Under God's direction, he ate, slept, and rested until he recuperated and was renewed spiritually.

To be consistently effective in intercession we need to take care of our physical body. Our body is the temple of the Holy Ghost and is an instrument that the Lord uses to carry on His work on earth.

We should try to maintain good health habits such as proper rest and regular hours of sleeping. Good nutrition and healthful eating habits are necessary for stamina and proper bodily functions. Food is the fuel that replenishes our body's cells, and sleep is the way the body renews itself. Daily exercise is also important. It increases stamina, and the end result is that we can do more for the Lord.

Failure to handle stress can be a killer in several different ways. When we have a prayer burden, we need to pray about it and give it to the Lord. We should not become anxious, stressful, or worried about it, but in faith and trust give it to Jesus.

At one time I was thinking about selling my rifles and shotguns. Although I like to hunt and spend time outdoors, I felt bad about spending time away from the work of God. An older minister advised me to not give up hunting, because I needed an occasional rest and diversion to renew myself and relax awhile. He helped me to understand that God does not mind for us to take a little leisure time to recharge our emotional batteries.

In the spiritual realm we need renewal also. As we pray for others and pour out our soul, we must have a spiritual intake also. We must allow ample prayer time for praise, worship, and thanksgiving. Worship is loving the Lord, and it is vital to our relationship with Him.

A husband and wife may devote much attention to their children's needs and neglect their own relationship. Parents unselfishly give of themselves and their time for their children, but they must also set aside time to renew their relationship with each other. That renewal is vital to the well-being of the family unit. The same is true of our relationship with God. We must not neglect the relationship of fellowship and affection for the Lord but take the proper time to praise and adore Him.

This personal edification gives us a feeling of security in our walk with God. We need this renewal to maintain our walk with Him. In turn we will store up the reserve strength to intercede again for others. "The joy of the LORD is your strength" (Nehemiah 8:10).

We should not wait until we are spiritually drained and exhausted before becoming renewed. We should renew the inward person day by day (II Corinthians 4:16). As an analogy, we do not wait until we are near starvation before we eat, but we go to the dinner table regularly. When we intercede for others, we should give a portion of that prayer time for worship and renewal. In this way we can maintain spiritual vitality so that we can be of more service to the kingdom of God.

Even though Jesus Christ was God manifested in the flesh, as a man He grew weary and tired. When He was tempted of the devil after fasting for forty days and nights, angels came and ministered to Him. In Gethsemane as He faced the ordeal ahead of Him, He prayed, and when He finished, an angel strengthened Him (Luke 22:43).

As children of the Lord who are filled with His Spirit, it is possible that when we give of ourselves freely in intercession the Lord may send angels to strengthen and encourage us.

The priests of the Old Testament received nourishment and strength from the showbread, enabling them to carry out their duties. We can find spiritual and emotional renewal in the Word of God, the bread of life, when we are fatigued. It will give us strength for the journey.

Chapter Thirteen

Prayer Warriors

The word *warrior* may summon mental images of a gladiator in a Roman arena fighting for his life, a brown-skinned Indian in battle attire seated astride a painted horse, or a Marine in full battle gear sloshing through a tropical swamp warily looking for the enemy concealed in the foliage. But some warriors will never receive the Bronze Cluster, Purple Heart, or the accolades of a homecoming parade down Main Street. Their battles are not fought with hand grenades, flamethrowers, or howitzers. Their enemies are not people who live inside different geographical borders.

Their battles are fought with spiritual weaponry. They do not fight for earthly principles, ideals, or territorial boundaries, but they fight for the souls of men and women, boys and girls. Their enemies are evil spirits and the sins that destroy the souls of humanity.

These warriors were not chosen to do battle because of physical stature or ability. They were not picked because of mental ability to plan battle strategy.

Prayer warriors come from all walks of life and from every tribe, kindred, and nation. They range from the young child to the high school teenager to the grandmother in her rocking chair. They are salesmen, preachers, housewives, painters, carpenters, truck drivers, and architects.

These are the ones who by the power of God through intercession cause things to happen. They cause demons to flee by their effective praying as the Spirit of God routs the enemy.

If a local assembly has some prayer warriors, the pastor is a very blessed and fortunate person, for without a solid base of prayer warriors his task of evangelizing a city is made more difficult.

As a young pastor in 1970, I was struggling to gain a spiritual beachhead in our city. There was just a handful of us worshiping in a storefront building as we began a home missions church. The Lord moved in a young couple and a single Navy man who began to unite with us in prayer. We began a blitz of prayer and fasting. It was thrilling to band together in our small group for prayer meetings night after night with expectation mounting in our hearts. After a while the breakthrough came and souls began to find God. That revival spirit never stopped but is still continuing in that church today. Those prayer warriors made a great difference in those early days.

It is thrilling and exciting to a pastor to announce a prayer meeting and at the appointed time see the prayer warriors coming in the doors of the church and making their way to the altar. In a little while the sound of their voices begins to rise in a crescendo as they begin to do spiritual battle for God. The battle rages and God's troops hit the front lines of battle. The battles are won in the "trenches," which are the prayer rooms or the altar.

Calvary's victory was won in Gethsemane. Intercession's victories are won as warriors fall on their faces in prayer.

Sometimes the prayer warriors in a local assembly are in the minority. Many people do not relish the labor and toil that accompany intercessory prayer. As a pastor, I have announced a softball game on Saturday evening and seen a record crowd come, but then announced a prayer meeting and seen a response that was not as positive.

To listen to prayer warriors in prayer is awesome. They might be old and feeble, but the note of spiritual militancy and determination is evident in the timbre of their voices. I have been fortunate to have pastored some people who were prayer warriors. It was exciting to walk into the prayer rooms and hear the booming voices ringing out or groaning in travail.

America has an elite group of soldiers called Green Berets who are especially trained for difficult assignments. The Navy has a similar group called the Seals. The British have their special warriors called Commandos. When needed these special warriors are called upon to get the job done even where others have not succeeded. They strike fear in the hearts of the enemy, for they are known for their skill, bravery, and determination.

When a church is seeking God for revival and the enemy is putting up resistance, the pastor can call for God's "elite forces" to prepare for battle. The pastor can call for prayer warriors to unite in intercession and in fasting. The battle is the Lord's, and victory is on the way.

God's people are continually at war with the forces of evil. As members of Christ's body, we have joined ranks with the blood-washed throng of the church of God. Though the eventual, eternal judgment of the devil will be accomplished by God Himself, through prayer and intercession we can enlarge and strengthen the kingdom of God. We can push back the borders and boundaries of the adversary.

Each one of us is important in this conflict of the ages. God has included us in His master plan, for He has called us out of sin and brought us into the church. In Gideon's day, every man stood in his place round about the camp, and a great victory was wrought (Judges 7:21). We need to surround our perimeter with intercessors and warriors, leaving no weak links in the chain.

God wants us to have a spiritually militant attitude. The spirit of Caleb caused him to be ready to fight for his inheritance at age eighty-five. God does not want a cowardly people but people with a glint in their eye and the challenge on their lips, "Give me this mountain."

When I pastored a church that was comprised mostly of Navy and other military men, I was accustomed to those men having to go out on special assignments. They were supposed to keep their sea bags always ready in the event that they had to leave immediately. At times the base would go on alert. God wants His prayer warriors to be forever vigilant and ready. Whenever the battle cry is given, it is time to go into intercession.

We can expect opposition from the adversary. Warriors are accustomed to conflict. They expect a battle. As we seek God for the salvation of the lost and the needs of others, we cannot expect the enemy to fold his hands and give in to us. The Lord wants us to do spiritual battle with resolve and fortitude. "Watch ye, stand fast in the faith, quit you like men, be strong" (I Corinthians 16:13). "Finally, my brethren, be strong in the Lord, and in the power of His might" (Ephesians 6:10).

Satan knows that not every Christian is willing to sacrifice and engage himself in intercession and spiritual warfare. And he fights the ones who do become prayer warriors to try to keep them from this vital work. If a person enters into this kind of praying with the serious intent of being used of God, he can expect the devil to try to deter him in some way. But a true prayer warrior will resist him and persevere to victory.

There are some basic virtues, characteristics, and attributes that prayer warriors display in their walk with God. First, they are confident in God. The battle does not rattle or unhinge them. They do not panic when the enemy comes in like a flood, for they know that the Spirit of the Lord will raise up a standard against the enemy. The enemy cannot bluff them, for they know their God.

Their environment is the battlefield. They are at home there. They function well in the heat of the skirmish. Prayer warriors are content when on their knees in prayer. They are uncomfortable with a casual, leisurely lifestyle with no burden to pray. They are miserable when not carrying a load. They love to pray.

Their battlefront may be a particular place around the altar where they prefer to pray, or it may be in a Sunday school room somewhere. Prayer warriors usually have a favorite place in their home where they like to pray. There the carpet may be a little more worn from their knees where they kneel in prayer.

These soldiers of the cross do not know the meaning of the word *quit.* When others give up and go home often they will be found still around the altar seeking God. They use a second effort and more to persist in prayer. Their characteristics are courage, determination, and persistence.

They have studied the enemy and are not ignorant of his devices. They know what his weaknesses are and how he tries to deter people from prayer. They are aware that the devil is always stalking God's children, trying to set a snare for them, and they are sober and vigilant to be on the alert for his traps.

Prayer warriors are leaders, if not by teaching then by their godly example. The younger saints can learn from these faithful warriors. When the younger ones would slow down in praying, these warriors keep pressing on, helping to prod them along. Prayer warriors are an asset to a church.

Prayer warriors are unselfish, willing to give and sacrifice. They have the kingdom of God at heart. They sacrifice sleep and recreation time to intercede for others.

These veterans of the Cross know how to use their weaponry to win victories. They move in faith and confidence in God. They are not clumsy and awkward, but they have used their spiritual artillery many times before. Faith, the Word of God, the name of Jesus, and the blood of Jesus are in their arsenal.

They know God not just on a casual basis but in a real, personal way. They pray much, and their friendship with Jesus is real and genuine. They are able to hear from God, for as sheep they know His voice. They recognize the power that is available to us in prayer if we live a pleasing life in His sight.

No barriers that the enemy can erect can stop the prayers of God's prayer warriors. "The weapons of our warfare are . . . mighty through God to the pulling down of strong holds" (II Corinthians 10:4).

Daniel prayed to the Lord regularly. We could doubtless say that Daniel was a prayer warrior. He prayed, and though his prayers were the object of an attempted blockade by the enemy, he persevered to victory. (See Daniel 10:12-13.)

No one has ever yet or ever will exhaust the infinite resources of God's power to answer prayer. We are not able to comprehend what is the height, depth, or length of His abundant love (Ephesians 3:18). "Now unto him that is able to do exceeding abundantly above all that we ask or think, according to the power that worketh in us" (Ephesians 3:20).

The effect of our prayers can reach out on a Saturday night as an unsaved loved one goes to his favorite tavern for a night of frolic. As he seats himself on a bar stool behind closed doors and darkened windows, our prayers can follow him right into the bar. The prayer warrior through the power of God can penetrate the barriers.

A backslider may go to her favorite theater for a night to escape reality via the silver screen. She may feel that she has escaped the eyes of people and God as she buries herself in the plot of the story. But about that time a caring mother who is a prayer warrior may go on her knees in prayer. The battle rages. The effect of her prayers slips into the darkened theater as the convicting presence of God sweeps over the backslider.

A home missionary battles to gain a foothold in a new city as he begins a new work. The enemy has entrenched himself with fortifications to block the salvation of the lost that he has held for so long. But prayer warriors go on their faces, and the walls begin to crumble and fall in disarray as God brings the victory.

Prayer warriors need to keep praying. The gates of hell shall not prevail against the church. Our intercession will result in victories for the kingdom of God. Intercession is not outdated but is as modern as tomorrow. We will not get the job of evangelism done without intercessors and prayer warriors. "Not by might, nor by power, but by my spirit, saith the LORD of hosts" (Zechariah 4:6).

Chapter Fourteen

God's Trauma Team

The lone motorist settles back into the seat and relaxes with the knowledge that he is nearing his destination. It has been a boring trip across the desert since leaving Los Angeles early that morning. As he passes the city limits of Tonopah, Arizona, he knows that Phoenix and home are only another forty-five minutes of this lonely drive away. It is a hot summer afternoon and the mirages on the road ahead constantly tantalize the observer with a promise of cooling water ahead, only to vanish into oblivion as he travels down the road. With the air conditioning running high and the FM radio playing soothing music, the motorist is lulled into road hypnosis.

Only a few seconds of drifting to sleep cause the car to wander onto the shoulder of the road. The driver overcorrects and runs into the center median where the car, out of control, flips several times, ejecting him.

This stretch of highway is heavily patrolled, and shortly a Department of Public Safety officer is on the scene. He radioes immediately for a medical helicopter.

In Phoenix at Good Samaritan Hospital, a helicopter lifts off the pad and heads for the scene. A trauma team begins to prepare for the ordeal ahead when the victim arrives at the hospital.

The trauma team is made up of highly trained and dedicated medical professionals who spend their lives day after day rescuing people from the precipice of death. They know how to remain cool under pressure and are unselfish. It is not a position for the fainthearted, but a strong will and determination are needed along with a healthy dose of altruism.

The sound of rotor blades splitting the air is heard, and the trauma team prepares to go into action. Loading their patient onto a surgical cart, they rush him immediately into surgery.

Hours go by as the team members fight for his life. The long summer afternoon turns into evening and the dinner hour comes and goes as they work feverishly. Massive internal injuries and bleeding necessitate transfusions, but the patient loses blood almost as fast as they can give it to him. The scene is gruesome to an inexperienced observer. Blood is all over the floor and on their surgical gowns. Beeping sounds from various monitors and blips on screens tell the status of the patient and his progress to the team members. Beads of sweat on their faces, weary muscles, and perspiration-soaked clothing speak volumes about what is taking place in the trauma room and in the hearts of the team members. Finally after many hours, the patient stabilizes and the final suturing is done. It is now a wait to see what will happen.

Several weeks later the man, weak and pale, walks out of the hospital on wobbly legs. Thanks to the Lord and the efforts of the trauma team he is alive. Their fulfillment and gratification as members of the team come in seeing a life that was nearly gone saved.

Twenty-four hours a day, calls for assistance are sent up to the throne of God. At any hour of the day or night, God receives calls for His immediate assistance and attention. Some requests are not particularly serious, while others are dire emergencies. God is never caught off guard. He who knows the end from the beginning is well aware of events that transpire, even before they happen. The eyes of the Lord run to and fro throughout the earth (II Chronicles 16:9). He sees emergencies developing even before we have time to call for His help. For many of these crises He dispatches angels, or He takes care of them Himself. We would be surprised if we only knew the multiple times that we were saved from trouble and possible death when an angel or the Lord delivered us.

Nothing escapes the all-seeing eyes of the Lord. Neither is any situation beyond the capabilities of the Lord to handle. He is omnipotent and there is no weakening or shortage of His power. What seems at the moment to be an extreme crisis for humanity is an opportunity for a miracle of God.

In many cases, God works through a member of His body, His church, to pray when crises and emergencies arise. God can answer prayer independently of us, for He is sovereign, but God works through His children in many cases.

God often looks for one of His children who is spiritually sensitive. He looks to one who is walking in the Spirit and is ready to hear the voice of the Lord. He speaks to that person's heart on behalf of a certain need.

It may be a need for someone he is acquainted with. In such a case, his faith will be strengthened when he finds that there was a need and God burdened him to pray for it. God gets glory when we thank Him and testify of His goodness and providence.

But sometimes a person is burdened for a need when he has no personal knowledge of the individual in trouble. But because the person is spiritually keen, God can speak to him to pray in an emergency.

When a desperate call goes to the throne of God, sometimes it is a life-and-death matter. Immediate remedial action is needed. At such times, God will often impress the saint of God to go to prayer immediately. Often there will be a sense of urgency from God in the form of a strong prayer burden. It is a time for sincere, fervent seeking of God in prayer.

Sometimes the crisis is occurring at that moment, and by prayer it is arrested. That is why it is imperative to be spiritually sensitive and keen.

Other times a crisis may be imminent and God burdens someone to pray so that it will not transpire at all. We can cause a crisis to be averted by our prayers in these situations.

God is looking for willing vessels who will be members of a spiritual trauma team worldwide. A medical trauma team by their devotion can save a physical life in many cases. If we are intercessors, volunteers in God's trauma team, we can help in the salvation of souls in many situations. A soul may be hanging in the balance, and a sensitive child of God can go to his knees and help save that soul.

Help is available for us from the Lord twenty-four

hours a day. We can rest assured that if a need arises we can go to Him in prayer. In times of severe distress and trouble when we need someone else to pray for us it is comforting to know that there is a network of prayerful people in the body whom God can burden to pray for us. Spiritual trauma team members will pray for us and help support us. But just as we are recipients of others' prayers, we must also pray for others. Each of us must do our part in the body of Christ.

Just as medical trauma team members must be dedicated and live sacrificially, so must we in the spiritual realm. For the saving of a life, they will miss family outings and sacrifice sleep and other personal desires. Humanity depends upon them. Likewise in the work of God, we must be willing to be a living sacrifice in order to be an intercessor. God may awaken us in the middle of the night with a prayer burden. We may be involved in activities during the day when suddenly God says, "You must pray right now." When we make ourselves available to God, we never know when God may ring our number and ask us to pray.

A faithful lady in Phoenix years ago was used of God mightily in intercessory prayer. Several of her daughters attend United Pentecostal churches in the Phoenix area, and one of them told of an incident when they were shopping with their mother. A burden of prayer came over her suddenly and she told her daughters, "I must pray now. Someone is in need." Her girls gathered around her in a circle as she knelt right there in the women's clothing department and began to pray.

God needs individuals in His body who will desire to be used as intercessors, people who are kingdom minded and are willing to be spiritual trauma team members. We all pray intercessory prayers in our normal prayer life, and we use much of our prayer time to pray for others. But at times we need to go to an extra dimension of commitment and sacrifice and give ourselves to the ministry of intercessory prayer.

Intercession is not the limelight or center stage. Our efforts will often go unnoticed. Our hours of sacrificial efforts will take place mostly in our private prayer closet. But the Lord who sees in secret will reward us openly, if not here then in heaven some day. The rewards in heaven will be great for dedicated intercessors in the church.

There are rewards here that intercessors receive. There is a deep sense of fulfillment and happiness in knowing that God has used our lives in this avenue of service. It is a very humbling yet satisfying feeling. It is nothing that we accomplish within our flesh, for without Him we can do nothing; it is the Spirit of God that accomplishes the work. We are simply yielded vessels that God uses for particular needs. When we have done all that we can, we are still unprofitable servants, for we have just done what was our duty to do (Luke 17:10). But there is a sense of satisfaction in knowing that God has used our surrendered life perhaps to thwart a tragedy somewhere or to bring a revival in a country across the seas.

When I was a boy, my father pastored a home missions church in one of the eastern states. Much opposition to this truth was demonstrated in the community, not just verbal opposition but also physical. Late one night several men tried to blow up our home with dynamite. It was a very real threat and a scary time for our family.

Twenty-three miles away was another United Pentecostal Church pastored by Brother and Sister Wilford Blake. At the peak of the crisis in the early hours of the morning, Sister Blake was awakened by the Lord to intercede in prayer for us. Our lives were spared, thanks to the Lord. The Lord had a faithful member of His trauma team who prayed for us and we were kept safe.

God's trauma team is a group of dedicated members of the church who give themselves to the ministry of intercession. They wear no identifying badge and carry no membership card in their pocket or purse. Neither do they have a framed certificate on the wall at home. These are simply children of the Lord who have yielded themselves and made themselves available for intercessory prayer.

Chapter Fifteen

Partners in Prayer

Partnerships are usually formed because of a need that one individual cannot adequately supply by himself. By combining wealth, abilities, and goals, partners can achieve results quicker and more effectively. In the business world partnerships are formed often because two or more people share the same philosophy, ideals, or goals concerning a certain venture. Their common purpose brings them together into an agreement so that they may achieve their collective purpose. If they share the same dedication to their business, their task becomes easier because of the combined strengths.

A marriage is also a partnership. Ideally the marriage partnership is based on love and trust.

A partner is one who shares. In a partnership two or more people with similar interests and goals enter into an agreement. One partner may contribute much more than the others, or the contribution may be equal. If many partners are involved, each person may have only a small portion of the overall investment. They share the profits and also the losses. They share the responsibilities as well as the rewards. They share the joys and also the burdens and sorrows.

As partners in prayer we are bonded together with others in a spiritual venture. The end result of a good partnership in the business world means profits and dividends for the contributing partners. The end result of a good partnership in this spiritual enterprise is that many souls will be saved, and one soul is worth more than all the wealth of this world.

We must share the burden for the lost and the dying. It is not the sole responsibility of the Foreign Missions Division to carry the burden for the lost overseas, but all of us in North America can be partners in prayer for the lost on distant shores. Nor can we close our eyes and hearts to the lost in other parts of North America, for we are all partners in the work of God. We must intercede for the lost and needy all across our land and our world. We are partners and must share the burden of reaching the lost and expanding the kingdom of God.

Not only do we share the burden for the lost everywhere, but we share in the joy and happiness when revival breaks out, whether it is in our local church, another state, another province, or another country.

We can be partners in intercession with an individual who is close to us and meet together in prayer. The Bible speaks about two or three agreeing in prayer so that great things can be accomplished for God (Matthew 18:19-20). To agree means more than just agreeing on the same subject. We become partners in what we agree upon and we make an effort to bring it to pass.

A marriage companion or a close friend may become

a prayer partner. The partners share requests and pray over them, and their combined prayers increase the effectiveness of their praying.

In Arizona each pastor's wife each year has another pastor's wife as her prayer partner to seek God. Great things are accomplished by two agreeing together in prayer.

One of the benefits of an organization such as the United Pentecostal Church International is that we can be partners in several vital areas. We believe in the same message as the apostles, and we believe in spreading the gospel to the whole world. We can evangelize the world collectively where individual assemblies could not accomplish it. Being partners together for the truth, we strive to maintain a watchful eye on any heresy or worldliness that would seek to infiltrate us. And we are partners in prayer from one side of this world to the other.

The entire fellowship can be partners in intercessory prayer for end-time revival. We are an integral part of the success of this thrust. We share in the responsibility and also the joys and rewards.

For a number of years now we have had a program in the Foreign Missions Division called Partners in Missions. By giving in offerings each month, churches and individuals become partners with a missionary and his ministry. But the responsibility does not end with the offering envelope on Missionary Sunday. On the plaques that hang in our churches with the missionary's picture and name on it is a pledge of support not only of finances but of support in intercessory prayer. Thus we become partners in prayer. After having been a district foreign missions director for years, I have heard over and over the plea of various missionaries for support in intercession from us at home. Many of them pass out bookmarks as prayer reminders. They tell us that they need prayer support and consider it essential. They need financial support but also prayer support.

The effects of our intercession can be felt overseas as we stand behind our missionaries in prayer. Over a year ago I was in prayer one morning when God burdened me for the Allards in the Ivory Coast. I prayed for them for a time in the Spirit as I felt a heavy burden for them. I prayed in tongues and felt a strong anointing of the Holy Ghost. After praying, I sat down and wrote them a short letter describing what had transpired that morning in prayer. I received a letter back in which they told me of a severe crisis that they had been through. It encouraged them to know that God cared for them.

Brother and Sister Rodenbush were in Ghana in the 1970s and were going through a crisis where they needed help from God. Brother Larry Blake was pastoring in Cutler, Illinois, at that time and was in prayer when God moved upon him in deep intercession and travail. Every once in a while the name of the Rodenbushes would come out of his mouth, and he knew that God had burdened him for them. Brother Blake was truly a partner in prayer with the Rodenbushes and the work in Ghana in that prayer meeting.

The Foreign Missions publication titled *Global Witness* lists the names of missionaries for us to pray for on various days of the month. The Foreign Missions Division also has a Foreign Missions Prayer Band. In addition to participating in these activities, we should be sensitive to the voice of the Lord should He call us to prayer for a particular missionary at any time.

Brother Scism has related two instances in which God used intercessors at home to pray for him while he was a missionary in India:

"The first answer to prayer occurred when Sister Scism and I, along with five national leaders of the United Pentecostal Church of Northeast India, were traveling from Shillong in the state of Meghalaya, Northeast India, to the town of Silchar in Assam State, Northeast India. This journey was made by bus, and we knew it would be an all-day journey, taking us to another conference.

"We left early that morning and were thankful for a beautiful day. Being in a hilly area some five thousand feet above sea level, we were enjoying the journey as we bounced along the narrow and rough roads in this very uncomfortable bus. The bus was loaded with passengers, and the top of the bus was loaded with baggage.

"About one hour away from Shillong I was feeling a little sleepy when all of a sudden I was awakened by tremendous bouncing, and as I opened my eyes I realized that we were going up a mountain. We came to a halt on the side of this mountain and did not roll backwards, which was amazing since it was very steep. As we all climbed out of the bus very shaken by the incident we found that the front bumper of our bus had caught on the stump of a tree, and this had held it from rolling back down the mountain.

"We had been going around these narrow mountain roads when all of a sudden the driver realized in applying the brake to slow down in order to negotiate the approaching curve that there was no brake. He knew we could never make that curve, and going off the road would have plunged us to great depths over the side of the mountain. In order to save us from what could be a terrible accident he quickly took the bus off the road and up the side of the mountain. This was a miraculous escape. Not one person was injured or even scratched or cut to our knowledge.

"We waited there for two or three hours while help was sent for, and eventually the brakes were repaired. Late that night we arrived at our destination.

"During our next furlough when we were traveling in the state of Indiana we were asked by a sister in one of the local churches as to whether or not we had faced a particular problem at a certain time of the year. She told us how she had felt such a great burden of prayer for us to the point that she actually, in intercession, took hold of the leg of the piano in her room and agonized until the burden lifted.

"We explained to her the unusual incident that happened to us while traveling in Northeast India. As we began to check the time of her intercession, comparing it with the time of that particular incident, we realized that God had placed upon this woman a burden of prayer for us at the very time this near-fatal accident took place. It was absolutely thrilling to us to realize that thousands of miles away God had placed upon this sister a burden of prayer that no doubt played an important part in our miraculous deliverance. Truly God loves His children and cares for each one of us. How thankful we are for this dedicated saint of God who was willing to respond to the call to prayer!

"The second miraculous answer to prayer concerned the growth of our church in India. We realized that some type of change in the structure of the church might be necessary to encourage even greater growth in the future. However, we were not really certain what should be done in bringing about the needed change to accommodate the rapidly growing work. Before us there were two options, and we were not really certain which way we should go.

"At this time of great prayer and seeking God's face for direction, I received a letter from a friend in the state of Oregon. He told me how that in his church just a few weeks earlier a member who was normally very quiet and had little to say suddenly spoke up in the Sunday night service with his eyes closed as though he were in a vision. He began to proclaim loudly, 'I can see Brother Harry Scism in India. He is walking through the forest and before him there are two roads. He does not know which road to take. Let us pray that God will give him direction.' This man was trembling as he spoke under the anointing of the Holy Spirit. The whole congregation entered into intense prayer for Brother Scism. Little did they know that at that very time I was desperately in need of God's direction.

"This direction was given to us and we moved forward, knowing we were doing God's will. Now many years have passed, and as the church has grown rapidly with thousands being added every year we are confident that what was done was certainly done in the will of God. Thank God for a sincere layman who was led of the Holy Spirit in prayer and intercession."

To reach the uttermost parts of the earth with the gospel requires a strong home base of support through prayer as well as financial backing. We must expand and enlarge our home base through the home missions effort.

Across the continent of North America are home missionaries in cities, villages, and hamlets who need intercessors to be partners in prayer with them. By our intercession we can share in the joys and sorrows with them as they labor on the home front.

Since its first broadcast aired years ago Harvestime has had its Harvestime Prayer Band. Through it we can pray for the radio ministers as they preach to multitudes across this world. We can intercede for the musicians and singers that God will anoint them in their ministry. We can intercede for the hearers of the broadcast that their hearts will be touched with conviction. Thus we can be a partner in intercessory prayer with the entire staff of Harvestime.

The Spirit of Freedom Ministries has its Prayer Club to pray for those who have been delivered from alcohol and drug addiction or who need deliverance.

We have bonded together in our fellowship along many essential lines. Let us bond together in intercessory prayer as never before. We are partners in prayer. Paul told the church at Corinth, "For we are labourers together with God" (I Corinthians 3:9). He also said, "We [are] . . . workers together with him" (II Corinthians 6:1).

We are not only partners with each other, but God is our partner also. The Lord also is deeply concerned, much more than we are, that the lost be evangelized. He is concerned about the needs of His children all over the world. And so He burdens us to pray intercessory prayers. We work with God, and God works with us (Mark 16:20). We are laborers together with God. And the purpose that unites us comes from the heart of God Himself: it is the whole gospel to the whole world.

Chapter Sixteen

Intercession and the Mission of the Church

The New Testament church is a called-out group of people from every kindred, tribe, and nation who have obeyed the plan of salvation as outlined in the Book of Acts (Acts 2:38; 10:44-48; 19:1-6). They seek to follow on after Christ, embracing a life of dedication, separation from sin, and witness to others of the saving grace of God.

The church is not towering edifices with spires reaching into the sky nor magnificent structures that leave one breathless at their splendor, though God's people can surely use them to worship in. The church is not a social club, though we do enjoy one another's fellowship.

The church consists of people. It is living, breathing humanity whom God has called out of sin, redeeming us by His precious blood and bringing us through the miracle of the new birth into a new family.

The mission of the church is to win souls. The purpose for our existence is to win the lost to Christ.

The intercessor plays a vital and necessary role in the process of winning a soul. We may spend considerable time in witnessing to individuals, perhaps taking them through a home Bible study course. Much time may be invested in showing a person scripturally that the plan of salvation is for today. But intercessory prayers are vital in bringing people to a place of repentance. Nothing replaces the heartfelt burden in the heart of a child of God as he weeps and prays for God to save a soul that he is personally deeply interested in reaching.

Several years ago I had the privilege of being in service on a Sunday night at Life Tabernacle in Houston. Brother Kilgore, the pastor, told the congregation that he had been awakened very early that morning by the sound of a voice crying out, "Brother Kilgore, help me." He did not hear it over the telephone, but God allowed him to hear that plaintive cry for help from someone in trouble. He spent much of the afternoon calling backsliders and others on the telephone, trying to find the person who was in trouble. Brother Kilgore's tender heart and compassion impressed me indelibly that night, and I have never forgotten it.

Brother Doug Davis, who has ministered in New York for a number of years, was preaching a special service in an eastern state. The minister in charge of the service asked him to tell us about New York and its spiritual condition. Brother Davis stood there for a considerable length of time weeping, hardly able to speak. Both men exemplified the heartbeat of God, which is reaching the lost.

The church must feel the plight of desperate, hopeless, helpless, lost humanity. The intercessor feels the weight of the lost and prays for them as hot rivulets of tears course down his cheeks. Compassion causes him to become emotionally involved with others.

Intercessory prayer is not mild, shallow prayer, merely going through a prayer list, or simply calling out names in prayer without any emotional attachment or involvement. Intercession comes from deep within the heart and becomes a pouring out of one's soul before the Lord.

Jesus poured out His soul unto death (Isaiah 53:12). Hannah was so desperate that she poured out her soul in prayer (I Samuel 1:10). Intercessors live close to the heart and purpose of God. They feel the heartbeat of God.

I vividly recall the keen burden I felt as a home missions pastor in a major city a number of years ago. As I was driving down the interstate early one morning, looking out over the sleeping metropolis, a strong burden churned within my soul for "my" city. As a church we must never lose that sense of destiny and mission. God gives us that burden and sense of obligation so that we will intercede in prayer as well as witness to and preach to the lost.

Brother J. T. Pugh wrote in the *Pentecostal Herald,* August 1989:

> The passage Jesus Christ read at the beginning of His ministry described the purpose and mission He espoused when He came to this earth (Isaiah 61:1-2). His ministry has been conveyed to His body, the church, which has been left in place to extend it to the ends of the earth until the end of time. . . . Only people who have a constant, consistent prayer life relate to the tremendous passion that motivated our precious Lord from the beginning.

God's people must rise above the choking cloud of affluence in North America that threatens to blind us to the needs of the lost around us. Prosperity and materialism will drain from us our sense of purpose as members of the church. We must never forget our mission in life, which is serving the Lord and serving others. Souls are our mission. The disastrous consequences of selfishness and carnality are too frightening to visualize.

We cannot shrug off our responsibility or dismiss it casually from our minds. God has placed this message of truth in our hands. Intercessors are needed to weep between the porch and the altar so that souls will be born into churches across North America and around the world.

I pastored two churches that were comprised mainly of military men and their dependents when I was young in pastoral work. Every two, three, or four years these servicemen would receive orders that could relocate them and their families to a different part of the world. I pastored these people during part of the Vietnam era, and I prayed for a number of them as they prepared to go to that troubled area of the world. They were disturbed and apprehensive, for they did not know what lay before them. Their orders symbolized a mission that they were sent on by the government of the United States. Some of them had security clearance for sensitive operations that they could not divulge even to close family members.

Our mission as members of the church is more important than that of any earthly kingdom or government. The Lord is depending upon us to evangelize the world. He has placed this task in our hands. Everyone can pray and intercede for the lost. Some will go beyond the normal realm of intercession and enter into a ministry of deep intercession for souls. But whether God calls us into a special ministry of intercessory prayer or whether we involve ourselves in intercession as part of our normal prayer life, we can all be intercessors in the kingdom of God.

Chapter Seventeen

Laying Up Treasures in Heaven

I had been asked to spend the night in an old house, an imposing structure near downtown Norfolk, Virginia, to guard it against possible intruders. My shift was from late at night until early in the morning after dawn. The house was furnished with beautiful furniture of a bygone era and restored to much of its former glory. One could almost see people moving about the house in clothing of the eighteenth and nineteenth centuries. In the library were old books with yellowed pages and faded covers of long ago.

At some time in the past this home had been someone's personal treasure. The beautiful silverware had been some lady's pride and joy. The period furniture had been used by the genteel people of Norfolk as they paid visits to the elite inhabitants of this house. But now those former citizens had been laid to rest long ago in a cemetery somewhere, and their treasures were in the hands of others.

We are building a spiritual house. We are saved by

grace and not by works. Nevertheless, either we are investing in earthly treasures or else we are building a spiritual, eternal house. Earthly investments are not necessarily sinful, but they are short-lived. Wise investments now can pay dividends later in the retirement years or aid our children's education, but heavenly treasures are eternal in their benefits.

Jesus cautioned those who set their hearts on treasures in this life, reminding them of their vulnerability to unpredictable and unexpected future events. A wealthy man could become a pauper overnight through no fault of his own or by making bad investment decisions. Circumstances out of his control could leave him penniless.

But heavenly investments are sure investments. There is no risk at all if one maintains his walk with God. He cannot lose. A person does not have to be wealthy and affluent here to be spiritually wealthy. He can be poor and lay up treasures in heaven. The return on his investment in heavenly treasures defies any imagination or description.

We can lay up treasures in heaven in several different ways. The dollars and cents that we give to the work of God if given cheerfully and not grudgingly will bring benefits here and in eternity also. The Lord will remember our labors for Him even though they may be done in secret and obscurity, unseen by others. No matter how small they may be, the Lord will not forget our labors of love for Him and His cause. Whatever good we do for a child of God from a cheerful heart will not go unnoticed or unrewarded by God.

One of the ways we can lay up treasures in heaven is through intercession for others. We can invest prayers in others, and God will reward us someday for our unselfish efforts.

Someday all of our possessions that we hold so dear will have worn out, rusted out, become obsolete, or been given to another. The automobile that we drove off the lot so shiny and sleek will be crunched, flattened, and recycled into another Ford or Buick. The new home will begin to age and slowly begin to deteriorate. Our clothes will go out of style and wear out. But our prayers keep on living and producing results. Intercessory prayers invested in the lives of others keep on living because they are invested in souls that will live forever in eternity. And God will reward us throughout eternity with rewards unknown to us now.

The only personal possessions we can take to heaven with us other than our own souls are our children. Surely it is reasonable to invest much prayer in their lives. When we intercede for the lost, we should also include the little ones who mean so much to us. We love them dearly, so let us lay up treasures in heaven by investing our prayers in them. Praying for our children is intercession.

When Israel prepared to leave Egypt they would not leave their little ones behind. They said, "We will go with our young and with our old, with our sons and with our daughters" (Exodus 10:9).

People save and invest money to pay for their children's education. Many thousands of dollars are needed to attend some of the more notable universities, but parents will gladly spend and sacrifice because of love. Let us invest prayer in our children and other loved ones. It will pay eternal dividends.

As we pray for others we are investing our lives in people that we can deeply affect for eternity. As we allow the Lord to use us in the ministry of intercession, our prayers for people, some of whom are unknown to us, will reap eternal rewards as we have a part in their salvation and deliverance.

God is faithful and just. Anything we do for Him will not go unnoticed. If we seek the praises of people down here, we may get our reward now. But if we do what we do as unto the Lord, even though it is in secret, someday the Lord will reward us openly.

We should pray for our pastor and his wife, for they labor to provide us with spiritual food. The pastor studies, prays, visits, encourages, preaches, and performs many other services in which he pours out his life for his congregation. His wife sacrifices her own feelings and desires to unselfishly allow him to fulfill his burden. By investing our intercessory prayers in them, we bless ourselves as well as them.

We should pray for our brothers and sisters in the church. We are our brother's keeper. In some forests trees seldom topple over because they are so intertwined that they support one another in their branches and roots. By investing intercession in our brothers and sisters we also help to solidify and strengthen our own walk with God.

Investments sometimes demand sacrifice in order to bring benefits later. People will save a portion of their income to invest when they really would like to spend it now for something. But they wisely know that it will pay dividends down the road.

Intercession may be sacrificial at times. It may be physically and emotionally demanding. At times a prayer burden will take a tremendous toll upon a person. But taking time to pray when other things press us for attention is investing now for a heavenly payday later.

Intercession is being kingdom minded. Intercession is seeking first the kingdom of God. Intercession is denying oneself, taking up the cross, and following Jesus. If we lay up treasures in heaven, we will never be sorry.

Brother Lanny Wolfe wrote a song that asks, "What good has my life been? Someday I'll surely know. How many souls did I win? Eternity will show." These words place our priorities in proper focus. By being used of God in intercession our lives can touch many others for eternity.

Chapter Eighteen

Intercession and the Body of Christ

The physical human body is a masterpiece of the creation of God. The brain sends signals to various organs, causing them to function with precision and at millisecond speed. Athletes perform physical feats with flowing grace and artistry as their synchronized muscles work in harmony. There is a harmony between the head and the body when the various bodily functions are working smoothly. It is unfortunate and sad to see an individual whose movements are jerky because of scrambled signals.

The analogy of the church as the body of Christ is a beautiful one and teaches us many lessons about our role in the church and how to fulfill our responsibilities to God, the sinner, and each other.

According to Ephesians 4:25, "We are members one of another." Ephesians 5:30 further states, "For we are members of his body, of his flesh, and of his bones." Christ is the head of the church. "And hath put all things under his feet, and gave him to be the head over all things to the church, which is his body, the fulness of him that filleth all in all'' (Ephesians 1:22-23).

We become part of this body by repentance, water baptism, and the baptism of the Holy Spirit (Acts 2:38). ''For by one Spirit are we all baptized into one body, whether we be Jews or Gentiles, whether we be bond or free; and have been all made to drink into one Spirit'' (I Corinthians 12:13). The body of Christ transcends ethnic, geographical, and other boundaries. We are joined and knitted together by His Spirit and by our obedience to the precepts of the Word of God.

As a member of the church, each of us fills a role in the body as the Lord sees fit to place us. Just as our hands do their duties and our feet their delegated task, so in the body of Christ we all do our respective tasks. Just as the eyes, the ears, the nose, and various other members of our physical body do the jobs that they were ordained to do, so each one of us must fulfill our personal position in the body of Christ. No one can say that he is more important than another, for all are necessary and would be sorely missed if they were not functioning.

I had the misfortune years ago of having some serious trouble with my big toe on my right foot. After surgery on it and being out of commission somewhat, I was very appreciative of that toe and what it added to my balance and equilibrium. What affects one member of our body also affects the other members. When my toe hurt I hurt all over. ''And whether one member suffers, all the members suffer with it; or one member be honoured, all the members rejoice with it'' (I Corinthians 12:26).

For this reason, intercession for our fellow members

in the body of Christ is vital. A brother may have a specific need for which we can find no earthly solution, and we may be helpless to assist with our earthly resources. But the Lord knows the need no matter how severe, and when we intercede for the need we draw upon the bountiful resources of God to supply it.

As Christians it is our duty to intercede for each other. Sometimes a brother is in such a severe situation, such as physical illness, that he cannot pray for himself. As members of the body we must intercede for him with compassion and empathy as if we were the ones in need. We must feel his pain and heartache.

The Bible commands us to pray one for the other. "Confess your faults one to another, and pray one for another, that ye may be healed. The effectual fervent prayer of a righteous man availeth much" (James 5:16). There come times in all of our lives when we need other members of the body to support us spiritually.

At a certain time in my ministry I went through a spiritual battle, not a battle over a sin but a battle within myself and with the enemy over a certain matter. Around one-thirty one morning, as I walked the floor and prayed, I realized that I needed help immediately. I called a fellow minister and pastor who was a close friend and asked him to help me. As the night hours wore on, we prayed in his home and touched God. Even though I was a pastor myself, I needed another member of the body to intercede for me that night.

We do not stand isolated from each other. God did not intend for us to be loners, for we are brethren. A member cut off from our physical body dies in a short time unless it is quickly reattached surgically, and the spiritual body likewise needs unity and fellowship.

The same Holy Spirit that flows through our souls flows through every other member of the body of Christ. We are attached together to the Head, and we are not supposed to be severed. Of course, we can cut ourselves off by unbelief and disobedience and thereby be lost. But God's will is for each of us to be members of His body, and intercession is a vital means of helping to keep each other healthy and intact.

In the medical profession amputation is not the first option. Limbs are amputated only when necessary to save the patient's life and only after every option has been exhausted. They are amputated when they drastically affect other members of the body. When a brother or sister is spiritually sick, the members who are strong are commanded to bear the weak (Romans 15:1; Galatians 6:2; I Thessalonians 5:14). We do not want to see them amputated.

We are living in what could be called the throwaway generation. Many items are disposable, such as soft-drink bottles, flashlights, paper towels, and tableware. The throwaway attitude is also prevalent in relationships. The marriage bond does not seem to be as sacred as it once was. Quickie divorces make throwaway husbands and wives. Children live on the streets because their parents became tired of them, and senior citizens who seem to be in the way are thought of as disposable. But in the church each member of the body is vital. Instead of regarding a weak member as disposable, we need to intercede on his behalf.

Unity is beautiful. Each muscle of an athlete flows in unison, and the harmonics and overtones of a piano blend together in a beautiful rhapsody. In the spiritual realm, it is beautiful to watch God's people as they flow together in harmony to do the work of God. Let us intercede for each other so that each of us can flow together in harmony to do what pleases the Lord. When one brother is used of God, the entire church should glorify God, for we are all supporting members. Let us pray for unity in the body, for it is vital and necessary.

Our physical body has a wonderful immune system to handle invaders. When a germ attacks the body, white blood cells come to the rescue quickly and in great numbers. The white blood cells work to protect and restore the infected area. As members of the body of Christ, let us be sensitive to the needs of others. When the enemy attacks a member, let us marshal our spiritual forces and repel the adversary to save our fellow brother or sister. Let us be sensitive and responsive to orders from the Head, Jesus Christ, as He burdens us to pray for another member in need.

God has placed us in the body as He sees fit. He has given each of us a place to fill and a function in the body. Let us hold each other up in prayer so that we will all do God's will in this life and be saved when He comes for us.

Chapter Nineteen

The Sacrifice Factor

The word *sacrifice* causes our flesh to wince and shrink away. For many people in our affluent North America, sacrifice is a foreign and forgotten word, relegated to previous generations. The latter part of the twentieth century may well be known as a generation of selfish and self-willed citizenry. The spirit of covetousness and greed is apparent and widespread everywhere. Sacrifice is an unpleasant thought and totally out of most people's consciousness.

According to II Timothy 3, one of the signs of these perilous times is that people would be "lovers of their own selves" and "lovers of pleasures more than lovers of God." This attitude of selfishness is in direct opposition to sacrifice and self-denial.

I was a small child during the 1940s, when America and much of the world were involved in World War II. My father and many other members of our family circle were involved in the war effort in some way or other. It was a time of sacrifice for many of the American people.

At that juncture in history the American people were united and sacrificial in their thinking.

People who have lived sacrificially, whether for their country, family, or the Lord, remember those lean years. Though the memory of harsher times is dulled by time, they still recall many of the sacrifices. But generations who follow have a difficult time relating to sacrifice.

Nevertheless, one of the reasons why many of us today enjoy the benefits of the church is because of the sacrifice factor of previous generations. They stood for the doctrinal purity of the apostolic message when it was extremely unpopular and often were persecuted openly for their stand. They labored and built edifices for worship that are monuments of their sacrifices for the glory of God. Intercessory prayer and travail were well-known to them.

My family was saved in 1948 in Parkersburg, West Virginia, under Brother J. C. Cole's ministry. The dear saints in that church knew about the sacrifice factor.

Many of us have had the privilege to sit down with pioneers of the twentieth-century apostolic movement and listen to them describe some of the events of their lives. Sacrifice was no stranger to them.

Even in more recent times, many people in our ranks know much about sacrifice. The Scisms, Freemans, Sheetses, and many others know of sacrifice in a very personal way on foreign fields. And many have sacrificed in home missions over the years, digging out a work for God while raising a family and working on a secular job. Many of these soldiers of the Cross have worn out their health laboring for the Lord. Over the years many faithful saints of God have supported and sacrificed alongside the ministry in many churches across North America.

As we look at the present and future, we must rekindle the fires of sacrifice. We must present our bodies a living sacrifice. Sacrifice involves not only our wallet but also our time, energies, talents, and lifestyle. The sacrifice factor is vital in intercession and travail.

Intercessory prayer can be and often is sacrificial. When someone prays under the weight of a prayer burden, we can describe his effort as sacrificial. If God directs an individual to go on an extended fast to seek God for the salvation or deliverance of a soul, the sacrifice factor is evident. If the Lord arouses someone from a sound sleep to pray at three o'clock in the morning, some sacrifice is involved.

We do not sacrifice for the Lord in order to earn our salvation, for we are saved by grace. But we know that God will reward us someday for any effort that we put forth, even though it may be obscure, small, and insignificant. The motivation for our sacrifices, however, must be love.

When we present our bodies a living sacrifice, doing what our hands find to do, it is merely our reasonable service. When we toil until we are footsore and weary, we have done our reasonable service. We could never repay God for all that He has done for us. We will always get the best of the trade. He gave us beauty for ashes. When we have done all, we can still say we are but unprofitable servants. The sacrifice factor that is so foreign to our affluent, greedy, materialistic society is still the norm for a committed child of God.

Jesus warned us not be overcharged with the cares of this life. In the parable of the sower, some of the seed was choked out by thorns, which represented the cares, pleasures, and riches of life. (See Luke 8:14; 21:34.)

Paul described the Christian as a soldier and the Christian life as warfare. (See II Timothy 2:3-4; 4:7.) Being a good soldier involves sacrifice. A soldier does not keep anything in reserve. If necessary, he will give his all, even his life, for the cause.

Paul spoke of keeping his body under subjection lest he be a castaway (I Corinthians 9:27). He also said "I die daily" (I Corinthians 15:31). Paul practiced what he preached. He was willing to spend and be spent for the gospel. Paul knew about sacrifice, for it was his daily companion.

Jesus said, "Except a corn of wheat fall into the ground and die, it abideth alone: but if it die, it bringeth forth much fruit" (John 12:24). Then He said, "If any man serve me, let him follow me" (John 12:26). The actions of Jesus vividly demonstrate the call to commitment and sacrifice. Gethsemane, the trial, the scourging post, and Calvary all cause us to bow our heads at His sacrifice, which far surpasses any of ours.

The epitome of suffering and sacrifice took place on Calvary's lonely brow when Jesus was brutally crucified. When we think of sacrifice, our minds are inevitably drawn to Calvary.

And we are asked to take up our cross and follow Him if we are to be His disciples—not necessarily to take up a physical cross and die as a martyr but to give our lives as a living sacrifice. If we are ever called upon to lay down our lives for the gospel, He will give us grace to do it, but we need grace today to live for God.

The sacrifice factor is a vital part of our motivation

to intercessory prayer. Our love for God and our commitment to Him will help us overcome the fleshly tendencies to be selfish and enable us to be intercessors for others.

Intercession can be very strenuous and taxing. The weight of the burden and desire may drain a person physically. Tears may flow like small streams down his face. But joy will come, and he will feel the contentment of knowing that he did not hold back but willingly gave himself in prayer.

We will never get away from the sacrifice factor, for sacrifice is God's way. We will never develop a more "modern" form of intercession. It will always be like Gethsemane, Rachel's cry, and Hannah's weeping. The birth of new souls and revival will come by old-fashioned weeping "between the porch and the altar" (Joel 2:17). We will never find a better way.

Chapter Twenty

Launching Out into the Deep

Some experiences are imprinted indelibly into our souls and for many years afterwards are vivid and real to us. Certain events surrounding our families and friends are woven into the fabric of our memory and are forever a part of us. There are also such times in our spiritual walk when the Lord touched us in a very special way.

Such an experience happened to me in the spring of 1974. I was pastoring a small church in Burleson, Texas, and working at a sales job in nearby Fort Worth. It was my practice to leave the office shortly after eight o'clock, go to a large cafeteria nearby to get coffee, and have a time of reflection and meditation with the Lord. It was my quiet time with the Lord, for the restaurant was not busy and it afforded a place to be almost alone before the hustle and bustle of the day.

One day, in a distinctive, still, small voice the Lord reminded me of the following passage of Scripture: "Now when he had left speaking, he said unto Simon, Launch out into the deep, and let down your nets for a draught.

And Simon answering said unto him, Master, we have toiled all the night, and have taken nothing: nevertheless at thy word I will let down the net" (Luke 5:4-5). The Lord dealt with me to enter into a deeper life of prayer. From that experience I reached a new depth in prayer over a period of time as I began to learn more and more about intercessory prayer. I do not think that I have arrived yet; I still feel inadequate and that I am in kindergarten in the school of prayer.

This kind of experience is happening to many of us across our vast fellowship. Ministers and laity alike are feeling the direction of the Lord to launch out into the deep into a fuller prayer life.

We cannot do the work of God in the shallows alone. We need to get out into waters deep enough to swim in as Ezekiel was commanded. We have the safeguards of the Word of God to keep us doctrinally sound and pure, but we need the power of God to reach this generation. Only by His Spirit can we accomplish the awesome task of evangelism, and we can do so by launching out into the depths of prayer. The early church made prayer a priority, and intercession was normal for them. Our pioneers of the twentieth century have told us that prayer was their lifeline. We must pray also.

The prophetic picture is unfolding. It is clear that we are running out of time. What we are going to do, we must do quickly.

The Lord will use those who make themselves available to Him. If we desire to be used in intercession, we must yield to the gentle pleadings of the Holy Ghost. Whether we are young or old, male or female, preacher or saint, educated or illiterate, God will use us to do His work.

After someone has walked into the depths of prayer his life will be forever altered. After he has been used of God in intercession and travail, he will not be satisfied in the shallows anymore. Few experiences in life revolutionize us, for we are creatures of habit and change slowly. The new birth revolutionized us, and we can point to certain sermons or services that touched us greatly, but on the whole we change gradually. But a person is never the same after God begins to use him in the ministry of intercessory prayer.

Being used of God in prayer does not exempt a person from the need for spiritual leadership. A local church member should continue to follow the guidance of his pastor.

If he does, he can be a tremendous blessing to his church as he yields to God in intercessory prayer. He can help to hold up the hands of his pastor and assist in the harvesting of souls. He should be humbled by the knowledge that the Lord is using his life to touch others.

Some time ago I was awakened late at night from a sound sleep. The Lord spoke to me one word: "Come." Then He brought to my mind the experience of Simon Peter as Jesus beckoned Peter to come out of the boat and walk to Him on the water. Again the Lord was coaxing me to enter into a deeper prayer life. I believe the Lord is telling the members of His body today to come and launch out into the depths of prayer as never before.

Any efforts that we make to pray will be met with opposition and resistance from the enemy. As we purpose in our hearts to pray more, he will try to stonewall and sidetrack us. If we are determined to proceed, however, and have a strong desire to be used of God, we will persevere and be victorious.

Let us not wait for a more convenient time, but let us act now. The Lord is counting on us and He needs us. Let us join the swelling ranks of the intercessors.